I was Thinking the other day About...

PONDERING LIFE THROUGH THE EYES
AND HEART OF A CHRISTIAN MAN

BILL JONES

I Was Thinking the Other Day About...

Copyright © 2014 Bill Jones
Published by Observation Publishing, Brooklet, GA.
All rights reserved.

Scripture marked (KJV) is taken from the
King James Version.

Scripture marked (NKJV) is taken from the New King James Version®. Copyright © 1982 by Thomas Nelson, Inc. Used by permission. All rights reserved.

Scripture quotations marked (ESV) are from
The Holy Bible, English Standard Version® (ESV®),
copyright © 2001 by Crossway, a publishing ministry of Good
News Publishers. Used by permission.
All rights reserved.

ISBN-13: 978-0-9904751-0-1

Dedication

As you read these stories, you'll see many references to "my wife, Sharon." It will be clear how important her encouragement and love are to my writing (and to all of my life). Thus, it's only right that I dedicate this book to my wife, Sharon – the love of my life.

Contents

Acknowledgements ix

Introduction xi

POP! CLUNK! 1

Words Like Thrusts of a Sword 7

The Patience of Toads 9

Pondering My Garden,
and King Nebuchadnezzar 13

Pick Christ's Heart 19

Open Paths 23

Comfort Food and God's Love:
Hot Stuff in Bowls. 25

The Girl with Green Hair 29

The Fruitful Tree. 33

Funny Put-downs? 37

Cue Marks 41

The Braves' Perfect Season 45

Blueberry Frame Art 49

I Was Thinking the Other Day About...

100 Years from Now 53

A Psalm for Today 57

Black Widow Bite 59

*Driving on the Roads
with Others* 63

*Where God's Nurturing
Comes to Fruition* 65

Falling out of the Truck 69

*The Apostle Paul's Letter
Is in the Mail* 75

A Religious Tablecloth? 79

Revival Service Tonight 83

Rivers and Mountains 87

Celebrating Words 91

Summer Tanager 95

The Fragrance of Christ .97

Is it Two Miles or Two Miles? 99

Pursue Wisdom 103

Three Reasons to Pump Gas with God 107

Prime the Pump 111

Pigeons on Power Lines..................... 115

Pecans and the Ox in the Stable 119

Mystery Object 121

Lover's Leap for Joy........................125

Are We Walking Worthy? 129

Broken Glass 131

The Speeding Car 135

*As Charlene Darling Says,
Songs Can Make Us Cry* 139

Savor the Small Stuff, Too?...................143

Really, Really Bad Spring Fever 147

So Fast! 151

Please, Lord, Make it Real................... 155

Along and Along............................ 157

In Summary 163

More about the Author 165

Acknowledgements

I hope every page in this book acknowledges God and His glory and grace. I often think of Jesus' statement that without Him we can do nothing, along with Paul's writing that through Christ we can do everything. I know that without the Lord, this book wouldn't have been written.

In the introduction I mention the instructor of a leadership course I attended. I credit him with starting, and aiding an important part of my thinking process. His name is Dr. Ken Chapman, who prefers to be addressed as Ken. So, thanks, Ken. (www.leaderscode.com)

The cover design and interior layout were done by Tim and Elise Alligood.

I've had many people graciously encourage me in my writing, so if I try to make a list, I will leave some out. So, to all of you, I say thank you. Your brief comments, compliments, and "I never thought of it that way" statements that you made in passing, were just the right words at just the right time to keep me going.

Introduction

The course instructor smiled as some of us in the class rolled our eyes and let out a groan after he told us the assignment.

Write a personal mission statement.

We were busy men and women, mostly middle-aged, who weren't necessarily taking the leadership course by choice. If there had been an option to skip it, some of us would have done so and used the time to catch up a bit on the growing pile of work back at the office.

Now we had an assignment that would be a waste of our time. Surely, at this stage of life, we had decided how we wanted to live it. How would writing it out serve a purpose?

I heard a rumor that some members of previous classes had presented the Boy Scout Oath and Law as their statement. Since I had been a Boy Scout and a Boy Scout leader, I considered this possibility. Using those would complete the assignment easily, and because they are great statements to live by, I would fulfill the task in spirit too:

<u>Boy Scout Oath:</u>
On my honor, I will do my best to do my duty to God and my country and to obey the Scout

I Was Thinking the Other Day About...

Law; To help other people at all times; To keep myself physically strong, mentally awake, and morally straight.

<u>*Boy Scout Law:*</u>
A Scout is: Trustworthy, Loyal, Helpful, Friendly, Courteous, Kind, Obedient, Cheerful, Thrifty, Brave, Clean, and Reverent.

All the points are very clear and concise, certainly Biblically sound, with actions and attitudes to strive for. After a few days of consideration, I decided to adopt them as my mission statement. It was still early in the six weeks we had to complete the assignment, so I was free to forget about it until it was time to turn it in.

For some reason, though, it stayed on my mind. The choice I had made wasn't bad; in fact, I commend anyone who lives diligently by the Scout Oath and Law. However, I wondered if my goal should be more specific to my life.

Midway through the six weeks, I changed direction and started working toward something more personal. In spite of my earlier attempts to avoid it, I found myself thinking about a mission statement. What did I want to do, and how did I want to live? What was important to me?

I can't say I crafted a masterpiece in those remaining weeks, but I did finish before the deadline. The result wasn't earthshaking or eloquent, but was passable. I used more words than this, but it came down to these basics: I wanted to be a good Christian, a good husband, a good father, and a good friend.

I completed my personal mission statement on time, and read it to the class as required. I printed two copies, shared one with my wife, and left the other on my desk. I was ready then to save the file in the depths of my computer, slowly let other papers bury the copy on my desk, and allow the whole thing to fade into a memory.

Despite those plans, my thoughts kept returning to the words I had written. I pondered what I said I wanted to be, and the question always came up: "How do I do it?" So, I began the process of answering that question. As I thought about the events, memories, and observations of everyday life (hence the name of this book), I asked other questions: Is there a lesson in this, and more particularly, is it a lesson from Scripture? How does God want the lesson to affect my relationship with Him?

I consciously and subconsciously filed those events, memories, and observations into categories and eventually realized there seemed to be three points that for me covered most everything. Thus, my mission statement today is different from what I wrote those years ago. Hopefully, it's more focused and does give some answers to the "how" part:

1. All that really matters in life are God and other people. So act like it.
2. Do the right things—for the right reasons.
3. Pay Attention!

I was thankful when I realized the first point is a paraphrase of the answer Jesus offered in response to a question about the greatest commandment:

> *"Jesus said to him, 'You shall love the Lord your God with all your heart, with all your soul, and with all your mind.' This is the first and great commandment. And the second is like it: 'You shall love your neighbor as yourself.' On these two commandments hang all the Law and the Prophets."*
> Matthew 22:37-40 NKJV

As a Christian, I could have stopped there and taken Jesus' words as my mission statement. But, the second and third points expand on the "how."

We're familiar with the "shall's" and "shall not's" in Scripture, and we should be obedient to them. However, the Bible makes it clear that God wants our heart, not just our head. Our attitude in obedience is critical—doing the right things for the right reasons. The Apostle Paul said it well in this example:

> *"And though I bestow all my goods to feed the poor, and though I give my body to be burned (as a martyr), but have not love,*

INTRODUCTION

> *it profits me nothing."*
> *1 Corinthians 13:3 NKJV*

I added the reminder to pay attention because I am easily caught up in just being busy in this busy world we live in. I develop tunnel vision and, like a horse wearing blinders, I miss opportunities to do the right things—things that I should be doing out of love for God and other people.

> *"Seeing many things, but you do not observe; Opening the ears, but he does not hear."*
> *Isaiah 42:20 NKJV*

This book contains stories and devotional readings that recount some of the events, memories, and observations that have led me to this point. The purpose is not to convince everyone to adopt my mission statement, but to encourage the reader to begin his or her own journey.

If we pay attention and take a little time to think, we can see the greatness and goodness of God all around us. If we then take the next step and relate it to Scripture, we will better understand what He wants for us and from us.

I didn't arrange the stories according to my mission statement because I want the journey to be yours. Make it that, and feel free to sort them into whatever categories you desire. Enjoy some time thinking about ... God.

POP! CLUNK!

I haven't checked any store's toy aisle lately, so I don't know if paddle-balls are still around. But, even if they no longer entice youngsters with thoughts of hours of cheap fun, the striking sound from the Infamous Paddle-Ball Incident will remain in my memory for a lifetime.

As the name implies, the toy consists of a wooden paddle with a rubber ball attached by an elastic band. You hit the ball and the band stretches and contracts, bringing it back for you to hit again. The object is to hit it as many times as you can without missing. After a while, you improve until you get bored, or you find your hand-eye coordination is lacking, and you get frustrated. In either case, you look for other ways to play with the toy.

I Was Thinking the Other Day About...

Back when I was twelve years old, my favorite alternative use was to hold the paddle and turn around, letting the force stretch the rubber band until the ball made a large circle with me spinning at the center. I focused my eyes on the ball so it appeared to stand still while the trees and houses outside the circle went zipping by. There was no objective. The frozen ball and speeding trees just looked neat, and the spinning made me dizzy. I would eventually fall in the grass and lie there, as the earth tumbled beneath me.

One day I was spinning when the elastic band snapped, and the ball sped away. In my backyard, that wouldn't normally have been a problem. However, that day we were having a family get-together. My cousin, Vicky, was sitting in an old straight-back chair propped against the garage, and totally unaware of the red rubber menace flying her way. The ball found its target and "POP!" "CLUNK!" sounded, as the ball hit her head and then her head hit the side of the garage.

Before the sounds faded away, Vicky was out of the chair, running toward the house, and hollering and crying as she went. Other cousins, who were playing at different spots throughout the yard, dropped their toys and scurried after her. They were unaware of what had happened, but they knew from her cries it was something they did not want to miss.

Vicky's wails carried inside the house, and the adults rushed out to see who did what to whom. The two stampeding herds merged on the driveway, huddled around Vicky, and soon it seemed everyone was hollering and crying. I ran around the edge of the mob, jumping up every few steps in an attempt to see the damage I had done. All the while, I was yelling, "I'm sorry, I'm so sorry!"

My uncle separated the crowd, quieted the noise, and examined his daughter's head. The ball hit close to her eye so a trip to the emergency room was quickly arranged. As they scrambled to get her in the car, I was horrified with the thought: "What if I put her eye out!"

I spent the next two hours trudging around the backyard in agony. I imagined Vicky wearing an eye patch, watching with her good eye as they drummed me out of the family like a disgraced soldier.

Finally, I heard the car in the driveway, so I stifled the fear and moved closer. Vicky wasn't crying—a good sign. I gave a slight sigh of relief. Then I gasped, and my anxiety soared again when she turned my way and I saw the bandage over her eye. My uncle saw the terror in my eyes and assured me there was no serious damage. The tiny Boy Scout who had been practicing knot tying in my stomach started loosening them, and the thoughts of eye patches and drumbeats began to fade.

My father graciously waited for the anxiety and excitement to lessen, and later that evening took me aside. He rightfully scolded me for being careless. I had figured out my mistake as I made circuits around the backyard, so I continued to apologize and promised never to be so reckless again.

Nevertheless, there was another unspoken thought in the back of my mind. While I was genuinely sorry for the results, I was also sitting there in amazement that it even could have happened. "Wow! What were the odds of that?"

Out of three hundred and sixty degrees of circle, the rubber band broke at the exact point and with the exact speed to send the ball flying over fifty feet to hit a target the size of her ten-year-old head. Everything converged to make for the perfect collision of ball into head, and then head into wall.

It took a very long week for Vicky's eye to return to normal from the black-and-purple mess it became. By then, thanks to the short memory of kids and the youthful desire just to have fun, we were playing together as if nothing had happened. Everyone had forgiven me, including the innocent victim. I hope that now, many years later, it's just a fuzzy memory in Vicky's mind.

Nevertheless, I can still hear "POP!" "CLUNK!" as if it happened yesterday, and I have to admit

I still sometimes wonder: "Wow! What were the odds of that?"

* * *

What did I learn from the Infamous Paddle-Ball Incident? One point was easy. Never spin it with people around. The second took some reflection (not always easy for a 12-year-old boy), but I realized that in all my actions I should consider the possible consequences, however unlikely they may be. That evening, with the sounds of POP/CLUNK very clear in my mind, it was obvious that giving more thought to my actions would have been wise. Perhaps with more consideration, I would have chosen to leave the paddle-ball alone.

My focus did change concerning the consequences of my actions, but my education came at the cost of my cousin's physical pain and my anxiety.

That's the problem with learning by experience—it often involves pain for us and the people around us. The ideal path is to learn what to do before anyone has to suffer.

Thankfully, we have the Bible to show us that path. As King David wrote: "The testimony of the Lord is sure, making wise the simple" (Psalm 19:7 NKJV). All the life lessons we need to know, including the one taught me by a paddle-ball, can be learned from the Bible.

In Luke, Chapter 14, Jesus tells His disciples to

I Was Thinking the Other Day About...

consider the cost of following Him:

> "For which of you, intending to build a tower, does not sit down first and count the cost, whether he has enough to finish it—lest, after he has laid the foundation, and is not able to finish, all who see it begin to mock him, saying, 'This man began to build and was not able to finish'? Or what king, going to make war against another king, does not sit down first and consider whether he is able with ten thousand to meet him who comes against him with twenty thousand? Or else, while the other is still a great way off, he sends a delegation and asks conditions of peace."
> Luke 14:28-32 NKJV

Jesus' examples make a clear point. When we're making a decision, we should wisely consider the possible consequences. Take Jesus' advice, and in terms very familiar to me, if you seem to hear a POP! CLUNK! in your future, run the other way as fast as you can!

Words Like Thrusts of a Sword

Some things people say to us remain clear in our mind for a lifetime. In elementary school, I had a friend named Chris. I don't remember his last name, but I do remember it was German because the kids often heckled him about it. It was the early 1960s, so World War II must have been recent enough that there was still some resentment of Germans.

Chris and I were good friends and had a lot of fun together. Thankfully, I can say I didn't participate in the heckling ... except once. We were in the lunchroom, and some of the boys were going at it toward Chris. Trying to be "cool," I joined in with a smart-aleck remark. As the words left my mouth, my heart sank to my stomach. Chris looked at me and said "Not you, too, Bill!" Those are the words that, even fifty years later, are still riveted in my mind. What a sick feeling that was.

That could have ended our friendship, but I am grateful that with my apology, the passage of time, and my being very careful in what I said, we regained the level we had before the incident.

Even at an elementary school age, you can learn a life lesson. I learned that what we say does matter—it can help or hurt people—and helping them is the better way to go.

I wish I could say I never erred again, that I never allowed myself to be influenced by others or by pride or anger to speak a hurting word, but I can't. I do hope, with those words in my mind and the Lord working in my heart, that there have been far fewer than there would have been otherwise.

The Bible contains many warnings and commands about how we are to speak. God knows how easily we can let hurting words fly from our tongue. But, we can be thankful that He has given us the Holy Spirit and, if we follow His lead, our words can be helping words. And, that's the better way to go.

> *"There is one whose rash words are like sword thrusts, but the tongue of the wise brings healing."*
> Proverbs 12:18 ESV

The Patience of Toads

We often hear about the patience of Job, but have you ever considered the patience of toads? Our house must be located in prime toad territory because we have a multitude of the little critters that hop out from under bushes and other hiding places each night in search of bugs. There's a group that gathers under the light on the carport and another group that fans out across the patio finding the patches where the security light on the power pole shines through the birch tree limbs.

Two of the toads spend the day under the moss roses in a planter on the back porch. At night they scramble over the edge of the container, plop down on the bricks, and hop to any light that is shining through the glass in the back door.

The toads are not alone in their search for tasty bug

treats. If the weather has been favorable, meaning it has rained regularly, the green tree frogs also hang around, literally. They're the ones with enlarged pads on their toes that give them the ability to crawl up the side of the house and even stick to the ceiling upside down.

The tree frogs attach themselves to the glass in our back door and spend the night, waiting a short time and then moving, waiting a little more and moving again. They rarely stay in one spot for more than a minute or two, and then they impatiently move on in search of better hunting.

But, the toads don't seem to feel the need to do much moving. A toad can sit for an hour in the exact same location, waiting for a wandering bug to land in the few square inches in front of him that are within range of an outstretched tongue and a quick lunge. I don't know how many bugs that a toad can catch in a night, but apparently there are enough to make them fat and keep them coming back and sitting patiently night after night.

It's written in the Bible that God provides for all of his creation—that would include bugs for toads. While not realizing it, the toads do acknowledge that fact, and they trust in it by going each night to a good spot, sitting and waiting, and then acting when the opportunity shows itself.

Perhaps we could learn from the toads' example. God provides for His children, too, and gives us blessings and opportunities to serve Him, but we can't find those while sitting alone in a hiding place. We must first move closer to the Light, drawing nearer to God by studying His Word, communicating with Him through prayer, and exercising our faith through obedience.

During this process we shouldn't be rushing about like the tree frogs, trying to find what God would have us do. Instead, it requires patience like the waiting toads. God will lead us in what He wants us to do, but the timing will be up to Him. If we wait patiently and trust in His faithfulness He will give us opportunities. When those are presented, that's when we must act. If we wait on God and then follow His purpose and timing, we will receive blessings from above. And, they're guaranteed to be better than those that the toads receive!

"But they that wait upon the LORD shall renew their strength; they shall mount up with wings as eagles; they shall run, and not be weary; and they shall walk, and not faint."
Isaiah 40:31 KJV

Pondering My Garden, and King Nebuchadnezzar

I stood on the patio and marveled at the beauty of the flowerbeds surrounding our backyard. The brilliant white blossoms of the phlox stood out against the weathered picket fence that defines the back edge of the yard. The hibiscus was nearly eight feet tall and almost that wide and was covered in pinkish-red hand-sized blooms.

The angel's-trumpet near the edge of the carport, while not yet blooming, had stretched itself up nearly to the eave of the roof. Long tendrils of the guara held out small gold and white flowers and bounced up and down as the bumblebees did touch-and-go landings on them. Plants of all sizes, shapes, colors, and textures filled nearly every available foot of space.

Cardinals and bluebirds added bright spots of color

here and there, as they gathered at the feeders hanging from branches in the birch and dogwood trees. Even the butterflies joined in and added motion to the scene as they flitted from flower to flower. What a beautiful sight it was!

I could remember years earlier when the yard was just a wide expanse of pasture grass and weeds. Over time I had developed the structure of the garden and laid out the flowerbeds one by one.

The fence was one of the first additions because I wanted it to anchor the back of a bed that stretched all the way across the yard. Even though not skilled in carpentry, I tackled the construction solo. Trying to find ways to keep the posts straight and hold up sections as I fastened them one by one made the job interesting. After a good amount of fumbling without much progress, I fashioned various jigs to, in effect, give me extra hands to work with.

I cut one section of fence in half, added a frame and set supports in an X-shape to create the gate. I was filled with satisfaction (and may have even clapped my hands), when I hung the gate, opened and closed it, and the latch bolt fit perfectly.

A working gate deserved more than a dirt path through it so I later laid red concrete pavers to make a walkway to accent the entrance and divide the long bed in two. I fashioned frames around the blueberry bushes and the fig tree and attached netting to keep the birds away. (I didn't mind sharing the fruit, but the birds didn't seem to know when to stop!)

After discovering one frigid morning that a water tank will freeze, if left uncovered, I built the pump house with a gambrel roof and a weathervane on top, which added rustic touches to the backyard scene.

While I continued to work on similar construction projects, I launched a separate task to transform sections of grass into flowerbeds. The area was once a pasture of Bahia grass, one of the toughest grasses around, with roots that can reach four feet deep. (A farmer friend told me that fact with a sly grin as I described my struggles.) Because the roots were so thick, my tiller just dragged me along as it bounced over the top of the grass without digging in. That left me no option but to do all the labor by hand. I ended many work sessions totally exhausted.

While reflecting on the work involved, I could also recall the history of most of the plants.

My wife and I bought the oak-leaf hydrangea at a plant sale at the local university's botanical gardens. The seedling was only twelve inches tall with two small leaves beginning to sprout at the top. I had to nurse it along for a couple of years, but once it was established, it really took off. It grew taller and spread quickly to cover an area over twenty-five feet wide. It was also

I Was Thinking the Other Day About...

the mother plant for several others that I had divided from it and placed in the pine trees along the edge of the side yard.

Even though it wasn't blooming at the time, and I had no idea what the flowers might look like, I purchased the Pagoda plant at the Peanut Festival, held annually in a small town near us. I made the mistake of not planting it soon enough that year and spent all winter moving it into the garage on freezing nights and carrying it out into the sunshine the following day. I finally freed it from its mobile container and planted it in the spring. By late summer it had produced spectacular orange blooms nearly a foot tall. Sure enough, it looked like a Chinese pagoda, with each bloom made of multiple stems and flowers in layers that got smaller and smaller in circumference from the bottom to its peak.

Yes, as I stood on the patio and looked at the surrounding beauty, while remembering the years of work that had been involved, I could have shouted, "Look at this great garden I built!" However, thankfully, I thought better of it and didn't.

In the Book of Daniel, we read of the great Babylonian king, Nebuchadnezzar, walking in his palace. I imagine as he walked, he could look through windows and from his rooftop and see buildings, towers, and the great wall that was wide enough on top for two chariots to pass each other. Perhaps he could remember when there was nothing but bare ground where those structures stood. He might recall the steps of planning, construction, and planting as they built the hanging gardens for his homesick Persian wife. Gardens so amazing they were later deemed one of the Seven Wonders of the Ancient World.

He gazed at the city and said: "Is this not Great Babylon that I have built by my power and for my majesty?" At that moment, God showed him who had the power and majesty, and the King spent the next seven years living among the wild animals and eating grass like an ox.

As I stood there and gazed at our backyard, I thought of Nebuchadnezzar but didn't mimic his words. Not from fear of having to eat grass for seven years but from the realization that without God, I could have done nothing.

I praised Him for the beautiful plants and flowers and birds and butterflies that He created. I looked at the fence and thanked Him for giving me the strength to build it and the ability to think of ways to make the work easier. I thought of the years I had worked on the garden and thanked Him for the time, resources and opportunities He had given me.

That day I knew what the Apostle Paul meant when he wrote to the Corinthians that he had planted, and Apollos had watered, but God gave the increase (1 Corinthians 3:6).

I Was Thinking the Other Day About...

Paul was writing of spiritual growth, but in my physical garden I understood that, while I may have built and planted and watered, it was God alone Who, in His power and majesty, had completed it and made it beautiful!

Pick Christ's Heart

We pick a person's brain to gather knowledge, like picking fruit from a tree or using a pickax to dig deeper for hidden gold nuggets. It's helpful to learn others' thoughts and ideas because their experiences have been different from ours. Their knowledge and perspective may help us better understand a problem or answer a question we're wrestling with. Picking a person's brain allows us to discover what they know, and it may give a bit of insight into who they are, but to know them really, we must pick their heart.

Picking a person's heart goes beyond gathering facts. It means when they're speaking, we watch their expressions for signs of joy, sadness, or pain. We listen to the tone of their voice to notice if it trembles from fear, speaks clearly and directly from a deeply held belief, or bubbles with excitement. We ask questions because we care about the answers. We want to understand their concerns and joys, and share in them. We watch and listen closely to learn what makes them feel loved and to become aware of how they show their love for us.

Relationships—with our wives or husbands, our family, our Christian brothers and sisters, and others we know—grow stronger when we reach that level.

In Philippians 3:10 (NIV), the Apostle Paul wrote, "I want to know Christ." If we have the same desire, we will spend time picking Christ's heart. We do that by studying the Bible. As we go deeper, more of our questions will be answered, and we will better understand Him. We will know that Jesus has clearly shown His love for us by dying on the cross and that He has told us how to show our love for Him:

> "Then the righteous will answer him, saying, 'Lord, when did we see you hungry and feed you, or thirsty and give you drink? And when did we see you a stranger and welcome you, or naked and clothe you? And when did we see you sick or in prison and visit you?' And the King will answer them, 'Truly, I say to you, as you did it to one of the least of these my brothers, you did it to me.'"
> Matthew 25:37-40 ESV

> *"If you love me, you will keep my commandments."*
> John 14:15 ESV

These two passages point out that we have another responsibility in the process. Once we have picked someone's heart, we must act on what we have learned for it to truly matter.

Open Paths

"The way to keep a path open is to walk on it."

When you first read this proverb, like many of them (including some in the Book of Proverbs), it seems obvious and not very deep. Of course, the way to keep a path open is to walk on it. What's so significant about that? The significance is not in the statement of fact, but in our thoughts about what it means in relation to our lives.

When I first heard this, I thought of a path through tall grass along the edge of a lake. Here and there, the path veers off to a clear fishing spot on the bank. Over time, if you don't walk on it and keep it open, it will become covered with grass, weeds, and thorns. At some point, trees can even start covering up the clear spots.

Several other "paths" in life come to mind: the path between me and God, the path between me and my wife and family, the path between my house and the Church, the path between me and my Brothers and Sisters in Christ, the path of service, the path of obedience, the paths of righteousness.

All of these paths should be traveled constantly to keep them open. If we neglect them, they become covered in weeds and thorns, making them more difficult to walk. If we neglect them too long, we may find that trees have grown up and obscured the paths completely.

The mention of the "paths of righteousness" is meant to bring to mind the 23rd Psalm: He leads me in the paths of righteousness For His name's sake" (v3). I believe that tells us why we are to continue walking these paths to keep them open. Not just because they're "good" things to do. We are to keep them open for the sake of God.

All that we do should bring glory to God. Allowing weeds, thorns, and trees to cover the path we walk doesn't bring glory to Him, especially if it is the path we walk to God.

Comfort Food and God's Love: Hot Stuff in Bowls

It was near freezing outside, and the drizzling rain made the cold seep into my bones. That made it a good day to eat hot stuff in bowls, which is just what I was blessed to do! Breakfast was old-fashioned oatmeal (with brown sugar and cinnamon, and actually cooked, not flakes mixed with boiling water); homemade chicken a la king at lunch (not always served in a bowl, but this was, which made it even better); and oyster stew for supper (if that one's not to your liking, substitute your favorite chili in your thoughts).

The list of "hot stuff in a bowl" goes beyond what I enjoyed that day. How about homemade vegetable soup with ingredients fresh from the garden, or gumbo (seafood or chicken or whatever else you like in it), or beef stew? Just thinking about those can make my tummy warm up! No wonder they call it comfort food.

Comfort food tastes good, but also brings a sense of well-being. Many thousands (millions?) of bowls of hot soup (chicken and otherwise) have been served by mothers and grandmothers when their children and grandchildren had a cold.

The soup itself has no healing power (I realize there will be debate on that). The taste is pleasing, and the heat can clear your head and warm you from the inside, so you do feel better—thus, it is a comfort. However, the real sense of well-being comes from the understanding that the person giving you the soup loves you and wants to take care of you ... to help you feel better ... to comfort you.

The Apostle Paul wrote a wonderful blessing to encourage and comfort the Thessalonians:

> *"Now may our Lord Jesus Christ himself,*
> *and God our Father, who loved us and gave*
> *us eternal comfort and good hope through*
> *grace, comfort your hearts and establish*
> *them in every good work and word."*
> *2 Thessalonians 2:16-17 ESV*

Our overriding comfort is an eternal one given to us already. Jesus paid the price for that. But, also notice that Paul prays that their, and thus our, hearts will be comforted in the present, and God's love will affect our hearts for good works.

Hot stuff in bowls is good on cold days. The taste and warmth make it comforting. Nevertheless, it only becomes true comfort food when the love of others affects our hearts (as mine was that day when my wife, Sharon, prepared some for me). However, our true comfort comes only when the love of God affects our heart.

The Girl with Green Hair

The young woman stepped into the MARTA train car, spied the empty seat by me, walked over, and sat down. She was dressed nicely in a knee-length wool skirt (at least I assumed it was wool because of its thickness and the temperature outside) and a crisply pressed white blouse. A pair of medium-heeled black shoes finished off her business outfit. Since we were traveling toward Five Points Station in the middle of downtown Atlanta, I wondered what her occupation was and where she might be headed to work.

I figured I had good reasons to be curious. From the neck down, she was a well-attired professional person. Up from there, it was a different twist. She was blonde—or at least half blonde. The bottom half of her shoulder-length hair was colored green. In addition, two studs stuck out from her cheek like silver pimples. What a contrast!

I realize I'm conservative and always behind the times on fashion. And, I was definitely "country come to town" in the big city. I was confused about what my reaction should be.

Green hair and studs in her cheek must have little effect on her abilities at whatever occupation she has. And, more importantly, if she is a Christian, I can't see how they would affect how closely she is following God. (Although, some questions about her reason for the colored hair and cheek studs might reveal some areas to work on).

We didn't have a conversation. My observation of her "life" ended in a few minutes at the next station, where we both left the train and went separate directions. My only information about her was external.

When Samuel was examining the sons of Jesse to determine who should be the next King of Israel, God made it clear that the external things were not what mattered most:

> "But the LORD said to Samuel, 'Do not look on his appearance or on the height of his stature, because I have rejected him. For the LORD sees not as man sees: man looks on the outward appearance, but the LORD looks on the heart.'"
> 1 Samuel 16:7 ESV

If the young lady had wanted to know (which I am sure she didn't), I could have told her my first impression had given me pause. If, say, she was a financial advisor and sat down before me as her potential client, there would need to be a lot of conversation to convince this aging Baby Boomer that she was the right advisor for me. (Regardless of whether that's right or wrong on my part, it is accurate.)

But, if, say, she came into the church I attend, my response should be to look on her heart, thank the Lord for her presence, and welcome her with gladness that we would have the opportunity to worship God together.

The Fruitful Tree

This year the limbs on the peach tree in our garden sagged to the ground from the weight of the fruit. I picked peaches, enough to fill grocery bags full, and we ate some, put some in the freezer, and gave away many of them. Since there were still peaches on the tree, I continued that enjoyable process (especially the eating part!) until they were gone.

For several years, I let the tree grow as it wanted. Each year it added several feet to its height and eventually grew to over twenty feet tall. Some years it did bloom and offer some anticipation of fruit, but very few peaches appeared, if any at all.

Finally, last year I decided it was time to prune the tree. It had bloomed early, and the thought of cutting down all those "possible" peaches did cause me to hesitate. However, since the trees you see in peach orchards along the highways aren't twenty feet tall, it's safe to assume the best height for production is much closer to the ground. Therefore, I sawed and whacked away and ended up with a tree not much more than head-high with three large bare limbs sticking out.

Because I pruned it while it was blooming, we had no fruit last year. (But, we did have a spectacular arrangement of blossoming peach tree limbs in a vase in the living room for a few days!)

The tree grew well during the summer and put out new limbs. The following winter actually stayed cold. That kept the tree from blooming too early, and provided extra "cold hours" that peach trees need. The blossoms opened as the weather warmed. Rain was abundant in the early spring, along with what seemed to be an over-abundance of honeybees and other insects to pollinate the blossoms. All this led to a tree full of fruit with plenty to eat and much to give away.

Jesus spoke of God the Father being like a gardener who prunes His plants. He prunes those who are in Christ to help them bear more fruit. This may take the form of suffering or adversity, or it may be new responsibilities and challenges that take us out of our comfort zone.

But, the pruning is only a part of the process. While we do have the responsibility to learn and grow, thankfully, we are not on our own to produce the fruit. Once the pruning on our peach tree was done, God provided the needed amount of cold, heat, rain, and insects at just the right times. And, like His provision for our peach tree, as God does His pruning on us, we can be assured that He will also provide whatever strength and resources that are necessary for us to bear the fruit He desires.

> *"Every branch in Me that does not bear fruit, He takes away. And every one that bears fruit, He prunes it so that it may bring forth more fruit."*
> *John 15:2 NKJV*

Funny Put-downs?

Don had a reputation as a tough guy. He would move up to high school the next year, and I was a year behind him. The age difference (very important in middle school), and the fact I wasn't a tough guy, too, made us acquaintances and not friends. But, for some reason we started exchanging verbal put-downs when we passed in the hall. "You're so ugly…" "You're so stupid…", etc.

It started out good-natured, but as usual, the barbs got a little sharper each time. Then one day I hit a subject that brought no verbal response. The anger flashing in Don's eyes was clear. Since he was bigger, stronger, and meaner than me, that would have been a good time to stop. But, of course, I didn't.

The crowds of students that always surrounded us in the controlled environment of a school allowed me to keep my courage up. I stayed on the offensive in the following days and took his lack of response as a sign he didn't plan any. I didn't realize he was just being patient.

As I made the rounds at the school's outdoor Fall Festival, I spotted Don and two of his buddies. There was a crowd around, but it was unfamiliar territory and didn't appear to be a good place for a face-to-face "discussion." I headed toward the parking lot where I hoped to stay out of sight, but he saw me and followed after, along with his buddies.

The trio split up and worked like a team of herd dogs, cutting off my avenues of escape one by one, until they cornered me between two cars. I didn't know what to expect until Don walked up and quickly swung his fist deep into my stomach. I dropped to the ground, gasping for breath.

They laughed and started walking away, thinking it was over. But, it wasn't. My cousin, Jack, was at the festival with me. He had noticed my hurried exit and came to see what was happening. He was bigger, stronger, and meaner than all of us. As he arrived, he landed two quick blows to Don's head, and Don joined me on the ground. Jack pinned him there and literally made him say "uncle"!

After that, it was over. No laughing. No continuation of a scuffle. No threats about who would get who. Don slowly rose to his feet and the three tough guys left quietly. I could breathe again, so I thanked Jack for the help, and we returned to the festival.

I didn't report Don's attack. I figured he'd been punished enough. The other reason was the warning he had growled as his fist hit my stomach: "Don't ever say nothin' about my Momma."

Yes, I had followed the trail we see so often when comedians are putting each other down. It eventually reaches "Your Momma is so..." I didn't know Don's mother and certainly didn't mean anything I said. I was just spouting off words, words I had probably heard on TV or in a movie.

But, Don had taken them seriously, and that look of anger at the first one should have been a clear sign to put my ego aside and shut up. After thinking about his words and my actions, I decided I deserved the punch in the stomach.

* * *

The game of besting each other with put-downs often ends in a confrontation like the one between Don and me. Even when the duelists cover it with laughter, you often feel the edge. There is something with each statement that sinks into the target's heart. It may build up and come out physically, like a punch in the stomach, or worse yet, it may reveal itself slowly, with a hardened heart and a broken relationship.

I Was Thinking the Other Day About...

The Bible warns us to consider the power of our speech. Words can pierce like thrusts of a sword and make wounds that go to the deepest part of our being. Grievous words stir up anger and hasty words can show us to be foolish. Verbal put-downs can fit any of these descriptions.

Ephesians 4:29 gives us a final word on what place put-downs have, even if we think we're playing around: "Let no corrupting talk come out of your mouths, but only such as is good for building up, as fits the occasion, that it may give grace to those who hear."

I wasn't diligently following God in those middle school days, but I do believe He was already faithfully teaching me. I saw how easy it was to let a put-down fly in jest and watch the target's eyes change from laughter to flashes of anger. I found that my words not only hurt Don, but eventually came back to hurt me, too.

There were no witty remarks exchanged the next time Don and I passed in the hall. We looked each other in the eye, nodded and slightly smiled. Perhaps we were both considering the lessons God had taught us and decided that a silent nod and a smile were preferred over starting another duel where both would be wounded.

Cue Marks

My first real job was as a projectionist at the Georgia Theater in downtown Statesboro, Georgia. It was a while ago, back when theaters had only one screen. The same movie showed for three or four days and then was sent along to another theater in the circuit. I did get to see a lot of movies a lot of times! I memorized many of the lines from the good ones and suffered through the bad ones.

Projection technology has moved into the digital age in many theaters today. However, back then, the movies came to the theater in metal cases holding several reels. Each reel was loaded with twenty to thirty minutes of film.

There were two projectors in the booth. To start the movie, you loaded the first reel, threaded the film through a series of rollers and sprockets, and secured it to the take-up reel. Turning two knobs brought a pair of carbon rods in contact with each other, causing an electric current to flow. When you backed the rods apart, it created a bright, blinding light from the arc.

You switched on the drive motor, let it get up to speed, then opened the shutter, and the picture appeared on the screen. After checking the brightness and focus, and listening for any catcalls from the audience that indicated a problem, you were free to set up the second machine.

When the first reel was nearing its end, a small hammer would fall and hit a bell signaling the projectionist it was time to get ready for the change to the other projector. You checked the film tension, started the arc lamp and waited for the cue marks to flash on the screen.

Cue marks are small black or white circles in the right top corner of the picture frame (the color depends on what's in the frame so they stand out). When you saw the first cue mark, you started the motor on the second projector, and the film started running up to speed.

A few seconds later, the second cue mark appeared, and you flipped two switches to open the second machine's shutter and to close the first one. The goal was to make it so smooth that those watching the movie didn't notice anything. You continued that process, swapping projectors with each reel until the movie finished.

Those cue marks tell the projectionist to get ready and then do something. Similarly, the Holy Spirit gives us cue marks in life. The Spirit's cues are more flexible than those in the theaters because they not only tell us what we should do, but also what we should not do.

A certain person comes to mind and you think you should give them a call – take the cue and do it. You're in a conversation and a cutting remark comes to mind but you hesitate to say it – take the cue and keep silent. You notice that someone needs help in a particular way that you are capable of providing – take the cue and do it. You feel a sudden urge to pray for someone – take the cue and do it.

Just like the cue marks on the silver screen, God's cue marks are there for a reason and are to be followed. But, while missing the projectionist's cue may cause some minor distraction for moviegoers, the Holy Spirit takes it much more seriously when we miss His.

"And do not grieve the Holy Spirit
of God, by whom you were sealed for
the day of redemption."
Ephesians 4:30 NKJV

The Braves' Perfect Season

Even though they didn't make it to the World Series, the Atlanta Braves had a perfect record with me last season. They won every game I watched on TV.

Of course, there wasn't anything about my watching that helped them win. I took the easy way out by recording the games and then checking the final score. If the Braves won, I watched the game. If they lost, I deleted it. Early in the season, I skipped the opponent's times at bat and just watched the Braves' half of the innings. As the season went on, I compressed my viewing even more and only watched the innings that the Braves scored in. Although I did follow their progress (and lack of it) through the season, you can tell I'm not a die-hard Braves' fan.

The main reason I followed the "watch or delete"

method was time. Baseball is slow. A game lasts about three hours, and since they play nearly every day, that adds up. I had other things I needed and wanted to do, so the delayed, condensed replay worked better in my schedule.

Yes, I did miss some thrilling plays and the excitement that comes from wondering what will happen next. But, I also missed the disappointment of spending three hours watching a lost cause. I realize those are all part of the drama of baseball, but I made the choice to forgo some of that in the interest of time.

I don't know how well the Braves will play this season, but I do know what won't happen if I continue the "watch or delete" method. I won't learn much about the Braves' players. I won't see them play defense and watch how they react individually and as a team when they're not scoring runs. I'll miss most of the stories the announcers tell about the team members that give insight into the players' personalities.

I also won't become a die-hard Braves fan. Passion doesn't come from superficial involvement, but requires dedication to learning everything we can about something or someone, and striving to get as close to them as possible.

The psalmist wrote that his soul pants after God like a thirsty deer pants for water. Passion like that isn't automatic. It builds by studying and meditating on God's Word, praying fervently to know Him better, and exercising our faith in Who He is and what He has done for us. Each step we faithfully take to "trust and obey" brings us closer to Him. The closer we get, the more our desire increases, until we realize that our soul is panting after God, too.

It can be fun to have passion for a team during a sports season, but seasons can be good or bad, and they do come and go. But, a passion for God brings true joy and lasts forever.

"Now set your heart and your soul to seek the LORD your God;"
1 Chronicles 22:19 KJV

Blueberry Frame Art

A sturdy frame to support the bird netting around the blueberry bushes was the biggest present I received at Christmas last year. Some design and assembly were required, however. I decided nine posts would support it—some would be eight feet out of the ground and others eight and a half feet. I began work by digging the holes for the posts. After digging holes for a total of 21 feet, I decided to take a break and save straightening the posts for later.

As I walked away, I turned to review the progress. Some posts were catawampus to the inside, others slanted out, and a couple looked like leaning tree trunks growing up out of the bushes. When I reached the house, I told my wife, Sharon, to look at the sculpture I had made. I declared it to be "art."

I Was Thinking the Other Day About...

She smiled and said most people would say: "Come on, boy, that's just some poles stuck in the dirt."

She was correct; they would say that, and really "the sculpture" was just poles stuck in the dirt. But I reminded her that I had seen sillier things called art, and people had paid thousands of dollars for them. We decided it depends on who does it and who says it is art.

I can't claim to be an art expert or an artist. My engineer's brain leans heavily on the side of literal, realism. I've probably missed out on sculptures or paintings that would have been moving or thought provoking, if I had grasped the concept. And having someone explain it to me doesn't always help my perception:

"Of course, you can see that this depicts the struggle of man versus machine."

"Ahhh, yes. Thanks for clearing that up. I couldn't decide if it meant that, or you were making a frame around your blueberry bushes."

Modern art can have meaning and beauty (The Vietnam Memorial Wall comes to mind). But, there may also be confusion. That comes from what Sharon and I decided: It depends on who does it and who deems it art. The confusion arises because humans make the "art" and set the standards.

Reflection on human nature tells us several things:

Out of the many artists, some are insincere. They purposefully create silly things and silently mock those who declare them great works of art. They secretly laugh at those willing to exhibit or purchase them. And some of those who exhibit or purchase do so out of fear of being labeled unsophisticated—afraid to admit the Emperor has no clothes.

Some artists, motivated by only arrogance, strive to be shocking, and end by creating something repulsive and worthless. Yet, there are people who applaud their creativity and call them genius.

Art critics, museum directors, and influential patrons have the power to set the standards. Some use that power to create or destroy careers on a whim, simply because they can.

In these respects, the art world is no different from any other human endeavor. We often do a poor job setting standards. Doing what is right in our own eyes, which often means whatever is to our advantage. Confusion abounds as we try to decide who is sincere and which standards to follow.

But, the confusion clears when we turn to God and follow His standards. They are perfect and eternal, not changing on a whim, or following the latest cultural fad. His judgment is never clouded with the human frailties we're plagued with.

I Was Thinking the Other Day About...

In our actions and creations we can declare anything art. But, if God says: "Come on, boy, that's just some poles stuck in the dirt," that's all it is.

"For God is not a God of confusion but of peace."
1 Corinthians 14:33 ESV

100 Years from Now

The chorus of an old song by Lester Flatt and Earl Scruggs ends with the line: "I won't care, a hundred years from now."

Most of the time that phrase comes to mind on Saturday night after my favorite college team has lost a football game. It reminds me that, while following college football is fun and exciting, it's not overly imperative when considering the priorities of life. One hundred years from now, it won't matter which team won or lost a particular game.

As my home church, Lanes Church, approached its 175th anniversary in 2006, I thought of that phrase. Not from the negative, but with the question: What things that are happening today will matter one hundred years from now?

I WAS THINKING THE OTHER DAY ABOUT...

We can answer that question by looking back. In 2006, there wasn't anyone living that had been at Lanes in 1906. However, there were still many wonderful memories—memories of parents and grandparents, aunts and uncles, and dear brothers and sisters in Christ—these loved ones who had been around one hundred years before.

What do we remember about them? It's their faithfulness and their devotion to God and His church. It's their love of God and their love for each other. It's their struggles and the tears of sorrow shed for and with one another. It's the laughter and joy they shared. What we remember are the stories about how they lived their lives.

So what will matter one hundred years from now? It's how we live our lives today. Our faithfulness, devotion to God's church and love for one another should be good examples to everyone around us—yes, examples they will notice and remember.

But, far more important than that (and the reason those things are possible) should be in our example of loving our God Who gave His Son to die for us. One result of that is the existence of every one of God's churches with His people inside worshiping Him.

The glory goes to God for the fact that Lanes Church has had a long history. And, the glory also goes to Him for those churches that have had longer histories and those that were created last week. But, the true history of a church isn't about the buildings or programs, or even its size. It's the story of the people in the church. Through those Christians who have gone before us, God has given us a heritage to be cherished. We should always be aware that we are now a part of that heritage and that what we do today, if we love and obey God, will matter one hundred years from now.

> *"For you, O God, have heard my vows;*
> *you have given me the heritage of those*
> *who fear your name."*
> *Psalm 61:5 ESV*

A Psalm for Today

Dear Lord, sometimes I feel so tired.

In my fatigue, my faith dwindles.

In my fatigue, my passions sleep.

In my daily busy-ness, I tell myself I am serving You.

Yet, at times, at the end of the day I'm not sure whether I did.

But, then, You give me a word, or a thought, or a verse, or a song, or a sight–

From those around me whom I love or those around me whom I don't even know.

You give me an opportunity to recognize Your Holy presence.

And, I remember that I am Yours and You are my God,

The One I'm trying to serve,

The God Who does not tire.

The God Who truly wants the best for me.

The God Who will carry me and give me all the strength I need to serve Him.

In this, my faith is strengthened and my passions awake!

I will praise You, and worship You,

Oh, merciful and gracious Lord of all!

Black Widow Bite

My wife, Sharon, is the only person I know who has been bitten by a black widow spider. One day she took her sweater from the coat rack, put it on, and felt a sharp sting on her arm. She smashed her hand on the stinging spot, shook her sleeve and the flattened spider fell out. The telltale red hourglass-shaped marking on its shiny black body confirmed what it was. Sharon sealed her attacker in a plastic bag and took it with her as she drove to the hospital.

Everyone at the emergency room was excited because no one had ever seen, much less treated, anyone with a black widow bite. It seemed to Sharon the entire hospital staff stopped by to inspect the spider and the bite marks on her arm.

I was excited, too, when summoned from an out-of-town meeting to take a phone call. Sharon told the story and assured me the doctor said everything was okay. The antivenom was on its way from Atlanta and would be at the hospital in a few hours. Most important, she had no extreme symptoms. I trusted her assurances, but it was still a long trip home to see for myself.

The doctor administered the antivenom when it arrived that evening. Sharon spent the night in the hospital for observation and was released the next morning. Thankfully, the worst effects of the bite were the five days of mental fog she endured from the prescribed megadoses of antihistamines.

How did a black widow spider get in her sweater? I claim the dubious honor as the agent of that deed. It was winter, and we were using the fireplace. At times, I brought in pieces of wood and stacked them on the floor next to the wall. If you can picture the woodpile on the floor next to the wall, and then move your gaze upward, you come to ... the coat rack. Apparently, the spider hitchhiked inside on a piece of wood, crawled up the wall looking for a dark hiding place and chose Sharon's sweater sleeve.

Like most people, it wasn't our practice to bring poisonous spiders into our house. However, the one that got Sharon was sneaky. We didn't notice it because it was hiding in something useful that we often brought inside.

Spiders aren't the only sneaky things we need to watch out for. Every day we bring useful things into our homes through television, books, and the Internet. These can help us learn and grow, make us think, or simply entertain us. Most importantly, these media are powerful tools that can help us as we seek to be closer to God.

But, there is a negative side to the words and images they contain. Those that are blatantly evil are more easily avoided, but we might miss the sneaky ones unless we're diligent. Subtle messages can hide among the action, information, and laughter.

A scene can have a funny line, but the action may portray sex outside of marriage as not only acceptable but expected. Scripture can be taken out of context or given a slight twist to make a misleading point. Tolerance of sin (sin, as defined by God) may be constantly presented as a greater virtue than living by Biblically based standards.

As subtle messages like these sneak into our minds and find a comfortable place to settle, like the spider in the sweater, eventually they can harden our hearts to the truth. Proverbs 4:23 instructs us to be diligent: "Keep your heart with all vigilance, for from it flow the springs of life." ESV

We don't have poisonous spiders sneaking into our coats or sweaters anymore because I carefully examine

I Was Thinking the Other Day About...

all the wood before I bring it in. Perhaps that's the process we should follow with all things we bring into our homes.

Driving on the Roads with Others

At times when my wife, Sharon, and I are going somewhere, I find myself getting frustrated or impatient in traffic. Someone driving ahead of me isn't going fast enough; someone trying to turn left causes me to stop behind them; oncoming traffic causes me to wait to pull onto the road– you know what I'm talking about. Sometimes, when I realize my impatience, I'll turn to her and say: "You know, these people seem to think they have as much right to use this road as I have." She always knowingly smiles, which causes me to smile and lose my impatience.

Where does impatience like that come from? I'm not talking about getting impatient with someone doing something dangerous or someone delaying what they've committed to do. I'm referring to the impatience we feel toward others who are just living life the same as we are. As my statement above suggests, do we believe we have special privileges?

I do know that, through the righteousness of Christ, the children of God are given special privileges. We are able to approach God with our prayers and be heard. We have the wonderful privilege of not being under the wrath of God (chastisement at times, yes, but not His wrath). Through our God-given faith we have the privilege of calling out "Abba, Father" to God Himself.

But, does that give us special privileges above others in our daily lives—driving on the roads, or going to the grocery store, or waiting at the bank? Of course, it doesn't.

> *"Everyone to whom much was given,*
> *of him much will be required, and from him*
> *to whom they entrusted much, they will*
> *demand the more."*
> *Luke 12:48 ESV*

This verse can be referred to when listing all the grand and glorious things we should do to serve God. But, does it refer to things as simple as being patient while waiting for someone to turn left, or while in line at the grocery store? I think so. After all, we are to show Christ in us in all things we do. And, I have to admit, that often in those situations, that does require "much" effort.

Where God's Nurturing Comes to Fruition

Not everyone reading this may remember the 1960s TV show "Green Acres," and it's possible some others wish they didn't remember it. (It's still in reruns over forty years later). It was a corny comedy about a New York lawyer and his wife who move to a rundown farm. Oliver Wendell Douglas' dream was to be a farmer. He wanted to do something productive with his hands and hard work.

The comedy came from Mr. Douglas' trials and tribulations as he pursued that dream. At times, when others questioned why he didn't give up, he launched into a speech about what it all means as "you plant the seeds in the ground, wait with anticipation, watch the plants shooting up to the sky [or "shoosting" as his Hungarian wife, Lisa, said], and water and care for them until you enjoy the harvest of your labor."

I WAS THINKING THE OTHER DAY ABOUT...

Oliver just wanted to nurture something and have it come to fruition.

I admit to having varying levels of "Green Acres Syndrome" through much of my life (wanting to be a farmer, while not knowing much about it). At this point, though, I do know enough to realize it's hard work, that sometimes pays and sometimes doesn't. I'm thankful for my regular salary, a small tractor to bush-hog our old pasture every now and then, and a few raised beds in the garden to raise a "crop" or two.

While the "Mr. Douglas" plans have waned, I can say the basics of the syndrome remain. It's still a thrill to go through the process of planting, waiting, watching, watering and feeding, and then enjoying your harvest. I'm thankful my wife, Sharon, still gets a kick out of seeing her 60-year-old husband coming toward the house like a little kid to show her my handful of tomatoes or carrots. What a blessing as the nurturing comes to fruition!

I guess, the purpose of nurturing anything is to have a positive effect—to help it mature. The Apostle Peter wrote of the process of nurturing our faith:

> *"For this very reason, make every effort to supplement your faith with virtue, and virtue with knowledge, and knowledge with self-control, and self-control with steadfastness, and steadfastness with godliness, and godliness*

> with brotherly affection, and brotherly affection with love. For if these qualities are yours and are increasing, they keep you from being ineffective or unfruitful in the knowledge of our Lord Jesus Christ."
> 2 Peter 1:5-8 ESV

The verses before these explain that, while we work on this process, it is God Who gives us His power, and His promises that enable us. God is nurturing us through it. As our faith grows and blossoms, through His help, it matures into that greatest of all things—love. And, we know that God gets a kick out of seeing His children show Him the fruits of their work, as we love Him and love one another. What a blessing when God's nurturing comes to fruition!

> "His (God's) delight is not in the strength of the horse, nor his pleasure in the legs of a man, but the LORD takes pleasure in those who fear him, in those who hope in his steadfast love."
> Psalm 147:10-11 ESV

Falling out of the Truck

My uncle's old pickup bounced noisily along the dirt lane leading to his farm. My cousins and I sat on the tailgate and dangled our feet inches from the ground. We slumped against each other, exhausted from a day in the fields. But the freedom of the open truck bed and the breeze from its movement began to revive us. Soon we were shouting over the truck noise and laughing, as we pretended that we might push each other off the tailgate.

Sometimes we'd hit a bump and the truck's sagging suspension would allow our feet to scrape the dirt. After the first few times, we began to make a game of it. We inched closer to the edge of the tailgate and stretched our legs to see who could touch the ground the most times and let their feet slide the longest.

I Was Thinking the Other Day About...

It became precarious when we hit two bumps in a row. The first would cause us to stretch out and the second would bounce us quickly again, moving us closer to the edge.

I looked down and watched the dirt and grass between the ruts moving steadily by. We weren't going very fast so it wasn't zipping or zooming by, just a steady pace. I reasoned that if I was bounced off at that speed, I could just keep my legs moving and stand up.

At the next pair of bumps, I got the chance to try out my theory. As we hit the first one, we all stretched out, giggling at what we by now understood to be danger. The second bump was more of a hole. The tires went deep and then quickly came back to the top. That sent the truck's rear end into the air. With that, my rear end bounced off the tailgate, and when it came down, I was too near the edge to stop. I scrambled for a handhold but found none.

I whooped out a long "Whooooaaaa!" as I sailed off, and flailed my feet in hopes of remaining upright. However, my theory had at least one (and probably many) fatal flaws. The definite flaw was I had not considered the direction I was facing. If a mishap occurred, I would bounce off the truck backward. No matter how good you are, you can't run backward as fast as forward.

That was proven as my feet hit the ground. Rather than showing any semblance of uprightness, my back and then my head followed quickly onto the dirt. I slid awhile, came to a stop, and lay there in the middle of the road.

My cousins' shouts alerted my uncle to stop, and they jumped out of the truck and dashed back to see if I was hurt. The slide had torn my shirt and scraped my back. But, thankfully, there were no broken bones and nothing more serious than a large ugly goose egg from banging my head.

I thought I had everything figured out. I knew I was on the edge, but I kept inching closer. Surely my plan would take me through. If I was bounced or pulled or pushed over the line, I could easily use my own strength to keep straight. But, as I lay in the road staring up at the sky, it was clear that my own strength had been useless, either to prevent me from falling as I kept tempting danger, or to hold me up once the boundary had been crossed.

It's not unusual for us humans to think we're stronger or smarter or quicker than we really are. We often push the physical, the financial, and the workplace limits. Each successful dodging of disaster makes us braver and more self-confident. We inch closer to the edge, certain we can handle whatever comes our way. Then a certain combination of bumps hits us, and we find ourselves flying through the air to the ground.

I Was Thinking the Other Day About...

Sadly, it's also not unusual for us believers to walk close to the edge, relying on our own strength. We read in the Book of Judges, Chapter 16, of Samson and Delilah. As she asked him over and over how he could be defeated, he became more arrogant in his answers. Finally, Samson told her cutting his hair would take away his strength.

That night, Delilah had someone shave Samson's head while he was sleeping. When she cried out that the Philistines were there, he jumped up. He thought he would simply go out and defeat them like many times before. However, he found he had no strength. His hair had been cut, but the real problem was that God had left him, and Samson didn't even know it. He had toyed with temptation and eventually crossed the line. Samson quickly found that without God, his own strength was useless.

> *"Do not enter the path of the wicked, and do not walk in the way of the evil. Avoid it; do not go on it; turn away from it and pass on."*
> *Proverbs 4:14-15 ESV*

God knows our tendency to think we can handle temptation on our own, and He knows that we will fail if we try. His Word has many verses like these, warning us with verbs like "avoid," "turn away," "depart," and the one that expresses it most dramatically—"flee!"

We shouldn't be walking close to the edge. We should be running the other way. Our strength will not keep us from being bounced, pushed, or pulled over the line where temptation gives way to sin.

But, thankfully, God has not left us to our own strength. The Bible also contains many verses that promise He will be our strength. If we take the warnings to heart and trust in God's promises and power, we will find ourselves standing firm. That's much more secure than whooping out a "Whooooaaaa!" as we flail our feet and hope to stay out of the dirt on our own.

The Apostle Paul's Letter Is in the Mail

Did you hear that the Apostle Paul wrote us a letter? Do we look forward to receiving it? Can we expect a salutation like this?

> *"Paul, a prisoner for Christ Jesus, to 'your name here.' Grace to you and peace from God our Father and the Lord Jesus Christ. We give thanks to God always for all of you, constantly mentioning you in our prayers, remembering before our God and Father your work of faith and labor of love and steadfastness of hope in our Lord Jesus Christ. We ought always to give thanks to God for you, brothers (and sisters), as is right, because your faith is growing abundantly, and the love of every one of you for one another is increasing. Therefore, we ourselves boast about you in*

> *the churches of God for your steadfastness and faith in all your persecutions and in the afflictions that you are enduring."*

Obviously, Paul won't be writing us a new letter. However, considering how he might address us, if he did, can be a good exercise.

Could he give thanks for our faith and love? Would he mention our steadfastness of hope? What about our love for others? Is it increasing? Would he want to boast about us, or keep quiet?

Those questions make me uncomfortable. I know there are things I do right, by the grace of God. But, am I doing enough or doing the right things with the right attitude?

Becoming uncomfortable like that is good if we resolve to do something about it. Being convicted but not following up with action does nothing but make us feel badly. So, I would encourage us today to find opportunities to address the things we are convicted about.

Of course, our motivation shouldn't come from the fact that we might get a letter from Paul. Our motivation must come from our love of Christ and our obedience to Him because of what He has done for us: For "while we were yet sinners, Christ died for us." (Romans 5:8 KJV)

When the Holy Spirit convicts us about something, we should remember that God's purpose is not for us to get stuck just feeling guilty. God's purpose is for us to succeed in following Him.

Therefore, we should be encouraged in our efforts to address that conviction, because He will provide all we need in those efforts. We should be thankful and strengthened and "mount up with wings as eagles" for He has promised that He will give us His strength and His grace, and that will be sufficient for us to do whatever is required of us.

A Religious Tablecloth?

As my wife, Sharon, and I wandered through the local discount store, a "50% OFF!" sign caught my eye. I picked up a package from the stack and read the label: "Religious Tablecloth." I wasn't sure how you make a tablecloth be religious, but apparently someone figured it out. There it was on the shelf for sale.

I considered buying it and watching it to see how well it did in being religious (but, of course, it was only given that label because of the "Last Supper" design that was on it.)

Through years of helping Sharon decorate for Church functions, I have learned that you can cover up a lot of different things with a tablecloth, like a beat-up and battered table, a super-sized can of green beans, or an old, nearly collapsed cardboard box. Then, whatever you set on it, from a flower arrangement to a group of candlesticks will look good and you won't see what's under the tablecloth. I guess, if you put a religious tablecloth over something, it will look good and appear to be religious, too.

Jesus often condemned the Scribes and Pharisees for their hypocrisy. (He repeated the phrase, "Woe to you Scribes and Pharisees, hypocrites!" so many times in the 23rd chapter of Matthew that I think of it as the "Woe" Chapter.) He said they were like whitewashed tombs—beautiful on the outside but unclean on the inside. "So you also outwardly appear righteous to others, but within you are full of hypocrisy and lawlessness." (Matthew 23:28 ESV)

We Christians can also be guilty of hypocrisy, of hiding under a religious tablecloth. We might outwardly appear to be following God and even sincerely believe ourselves that we are. But, in the place where it counts, in our hearts, we may be envious or greedy, or in other ways sinful. While we may be successful in hiding that from others, and deceiving ourselves for a while, we can never hide from God. "...Beware of the leaven of the Pharisees, which is hypocrisy. Nothing is covered up that will not be revealed, or hidden that will not be known." (Luke 12:1-2 ESV)

God knows our hearts so there is no need to try covering up. The best thing to do is to be obedient to Him, search our hearts and confess our sins. God's

Word has given us this marvelous promise: "If we confess our sins, he is faithful and just to forgive us our sins and to cleanse us from all unrighteousness." (1 John 1:9 ESV) If we trust in that promise and rely on His power to cleanse us, we won't need a religious tablecloth to cover us. For what is within us will be revealed and be beautiful—a righteousness not from ourselves, but a righteousness that comes through Jesus Christ Himself! "Filled with the fruit of righteousness that comes through Jesus Christ, to the glory and praise of God." (Philippians 1:11 ESV)

Revival Service Tonight

The church sign read "Rivival Service Tonight." My first thought was the misspelling of Revival seemed to take away from the message.

But before I went too far along the negative path, it dawned on me that it was very good there was a revival service that night (spelled either way). Perhaps the person setting up the sign was excited and in his haste just put up the wrong letter. After all, a revival, a true revival, is something to get excited about. Or maybe he didn't have another "e" in his pack of letters. When he found he didn't have the needed letter, he could have just quit and not put up a sign of any kind. If it couldn't be perfect, why bother to get the message out at all. But, if lack of letters was the cause, he plunged ahead anyway, knowing it wouldn't be perfect and that some would look on it negatively. But he also knew that those

I Was Thinking the Other Day About...

looking for a revival would understand what it meant.

I realize all that is speculation, and it's quite likely that the person setting up the sign just misspelled revival. Church signs, as a rule, should be done correctly because misspelled words will reflect negatively on God's church. But, I'll also say a mistake such as this is not the end of the world. It should be corrected when found, and things should move on.

When it comes to getting the message out, the Church's people are much more important than the Church's sign. Are you excited about what God has done for you? Are you excited about the thought of revival? Do the people around you see that excitement? Do you keep quiet about Christ and your faith because you just don't know all the Scriptures, and you don't think you express yourself well? Or do you speak out, telling others what Christ has done for you in your own words and leaving it to God to have His message understood?

We sometimes get stuck waiting for the perfect time, location, words, thoughts, etc., before we tell the Good News. But we are called to speak out. The great thing is that it doesn't require perfection on our part. God will do the job of perfecting it in the hearts of His people!

After all, a misspelled word on a sign just gave us all something to think about and I don't think it's presumptuous to say that the Holy Spirit probably led us in many different directions with our thoughts.

REVIVAL SERVICE TONIGHT

"Come and hear, all you who fear God, and I will declare what He has done for my soul."
Psalm 66:16 NKJV

Rivers and Mountains

I heard an amazing fact in an oceanographer's presentation. He said if you combined all the water from all the rivers that flow into the Atlantic Ocean from North Carolina to Florida, that would still be less than 15% of the amount of water that flows through the Mississippi River.

The Mississippi and its tributaries do drain a huge land mass, but if we imagine combining the rivers we're most familiar with here in southeast Georgia, we would think of a lot of water! Then, if we added all the other rivers you cross on I-95 north and south of here, it seems that would be the biggest river in the world. But, it would still be puny compared to the Mighty Mississippi.

The Mississippi ranks as the tenth largest river on

the planet. However, if you consider the Amazon River in South America, the Mississippi isn't so mighty. The Amazon's water flow is greater than that of the next ten largest rivers combined, and it accounts for almost 20% of the world's total river flow.

Many of us have been in the Appalachian Mountains and know how big they are. Definitely the biggest around here! A few years ago, my wife, Sharon, and I were blessed to visit Colorado and see a portion of the Rocky Mountains. Movies and photographs don't do them justice. "Magnificent" and "awesome" are the words that come to mind. The size and height of the Appalachians pale in comparison to the Rockies.

So, are the Rockies the biggest mountains on earth? Not really. No peak in the Rockies even makes it close to the top 500 tallest in the world. The Himalayas, with Mount Everest being the highest peak of all at 29,029 feet, appear to be the champions. Nine of the top ten highest peaks on the surface of the earth are in the Himalayas.

But, if we look at those not on the surface of the earth, meaning their base is on the ocean floor, we find the real winner—Mauna Kea, whose volcanic "peak" shows above the water as the island of that name in the Hawaiian Islands. From base to peak, it towers nearly 4,000 feet higher than Mount Everest.

So why make this listing of geographical facts? I

want to expand your imagination when thinking of bigger, higher and other such words. And, I want you to think about God.

Higher than the heavens are above the earth are God's ways and thoughts above ours. Greater is He that is in us than he that is in the world. God is greater than all and no one can take us from His hand. Greater love has no man than this, that He would lay down His life for His friends—and we are His friends.

"Now to Him who is able to do exceedingly abundantly above all that we ask or think, according to the power that works in us, to Him be glory in the church by Christ Jesus to all generations, forever and ever. Amen."
Ephesians 3:20-21 NKJV

Celebrating Words

There are already some "word" celebrations in place, such as the "Celebrating Words Festival" in Los Angeles, "National Writing Day" and "I Love to Write Day." But, this will be on a smaller scale of just a few minutes.

Words are fun to play with. The sign says "Giant Tire Sale," and you wonder just how big the tires are. Or, you think of movie titles like "The Sum of All Fears" and imagine what the plot would be for "The Fear of All Sums"?

My favorite personal example came at a produce distribution plant. There were rows and rows of boxes stacked to the ceiling. A label on the side of each box indicated its contents. Most were straightforward (tomatoes, peppers, bananas, etc.); however, one

I Was Thinking the Other Day About...

box stood out. Its label read simply: "Squash, Do Not Crush."

I never figured out the difference between the two, and why squashing was better than crushing in this case. I imagine someone was just having fun with words, and it may even be a standard produce plant gag, but it sure stayed with me. I suppose I celebrate words each time I think of it.

As Christians, our celebration of words must include God's Word. There are passages that can be fun. Think of short Zaccheus climbing up a tree so he could see Jesus (Luke 19), or Balaam's probable reaction when his donkey talked to him (Numbers 22:28).

However, in our celebration, we can move far beyond fun, and we can consider the joy, thankfulness, and humility that Scripture brings us.

One of my favorite verses comes when Nehemiah is encouraging the people in Jerusalem to rebuild the wall around the city. He, in effect, tells them "Let me tell you the good things God has done to bring me to this point." Their response is "Let us rise up and build!"

Let us take that verse and celebrate what God has done for us.

> *"Then I told them of the hand of my God which was good upon me."*
> *Nehemiah 2:18 KJV*

Celebrating Words

"The Lord is my shepherd, I shall not want."
Psalm 23:1 KJV

"Then I told them of the hand of my God
which was good upon me."

"But Noah (and we) found grace in
the eyes of the Lord."
Genesis 6:8 KJV

"Then I told them of the hand of my God
which was good upon me."

"And she shall bring forth a Son and thou
shall call His name Jesus; for He shall save
His people from their sins."
Matthew 1:21 KJV

"Then I told them of the hand of my God
which was good upon me."

"For when we were yet without strength,
in due time, Christ died for the ungodly."
Romans 5:6 KJV

"Then I told them of the hand of my God
which was good upon me."

"For I am not ashamed of the gospel of Christ,
for it is the power of God unto salvation
to every one that believes."
Romans 1:16 KJV

I Was Thinking the Other Day About…

"Then I told them of the hand of my God which was good upon me."

"There is therefore now no condemnation to them which are in Christ Jesus."
Romans 8:1

"Then I told them of the hand of my God which was good upon me."

"Surely goodness and mercy shall follow me all the days of my life: and I will dwell in the house of the Lord forever."
Psalm 23:6

Those are the true Words we celebrate!

Summer Tanager

The red spot hopping among the pecan tree limbs caught my eye. I thought it was a male cardinal since we had an abundance of them. But, as I looked closer, I saw it wasn't. The bird's head was smooth, with no topknot, and no black highlight around its beak. It was bright red, with wings slightly darker than the body.

He flew to a pine tree and another bird popped out from a different limb and followed. That one had the same shape but a more mottled appearance.

I couldn't remember seeing this species before, so I did some research. I found they were male and female summer tanagers. Some interesting facts (at least I thought they were): The male is the only bird native to the United States that is red all over. They inhabit open woodlands in the southern states during summer

I Was Thinking the Other Day About...

and migrate to Central and South America during the winter. They are bee and wasp specialists. They catch the insect in flight and kill it by beating it on a limb. Then they rub it on the limb to remove the stinger before they eat it.

We didn't witness their wasp-killing skills but enjoyed a few days watching them around the yard until they moved on. I didn't think they left for lack of wasps because we had plenty of them. Perhaps they went in search of some open woodland. It was still Spring so it wasn't time for their migration.

It's always enjoyable when we notice something new (at least to us) in God's creation. The beauty, variety, and characteristics are amazing, and yes, downright awesome. The blessings of His goodness and greatness are all around us. We just have to take a minute and look and listen.

Hopefully the summer tanagers will return next year and remind us to give thanks to God for the blessings He provides.

> *"O give thanks unto the LORD; for he is good: for his mercy endureth forever. O give thanks unto the God of gods: for his mercy endureth forever. O give thanks to the Lord of lords: for his mercy endureth forever. To him who alone doeth great wonders: for his mercy endureth forever."*
> Psalm 136:1-4 KJV

The Fragrance of Christ

> *"But, thanks be to God, who in Christ always leads us in triumphal procession, and through us spreads the fragrance of the knowledge of him everywhere."*
> 2 Corinthians 2:14 ESV

Two thoughts on this verse:

We have large bushes of four o'clocks growing by our back steps. The flowers open in the late afternoon and give off a wonderful fragrance. It's not overpowering, just a subtle aroma that permeates the area. You can stand near the bush and not notice it outright. But, after a minute or two, you begin to sense there's something nice close by. Something that makes you want to hang around awhile and enjoy the presence.

I WAS THINKING THE OTHER DAY ABOUT...

The verse above tells us God uses us to spread the fragrance of the knowledge of Jesus everywhere. To do that, we don't need to be overpowering. We should look for opportunities to tell others about Jesus, but we can also spread His fragrance without doing that.

I think the best way to spread the fragrance of Christ is to show His love in all we do and say. Those around us should sense there's something nice close by (Christ's Spirit) and want to hang around and enjoy His presence in us.

As I thought more about this verse, another fragrance came to mind—women's perfume. Not all women's perfume is pleasingly fragrant to me. Some is too strong (or applied too heavily) and is overpowering. Some has what I consider a strange smell—but that's just a matter of taste.

But, I do have a favorite perfume that other women wear (other women being all who are not my wife, Sharon). My favorite perfume that other women wear is any that reminds me of Sharon. If their perfume is one that Sharon uses, the fragrance takes my mind immediately to her.

That seems a good way to spread the fragrance of Christ. Our actions and words should remind others of Jesus and take their minds immediately to Him.

Is it Two Miles or Two Miles?

When I give someone directions to our house from the nearest town, I tell them to turn left at the four-way stop at Mud Road and Arcola Road, and then go two miles on Mud Road to M.P. Martin Road. That seems clear, but often I get calls saying they can't find it.

They've gotten the Mud Road part right, but they've either gone too far or not far enough to find M.P. Martin Road. I think the confusion comes from me saying the distance is two miles—not because it isn't two miles, but because it is two miles.

It's not a little over or a little under two miles; it's not around two miles; it's not "go about two miles and start looking for it." It's two miles.

I think it's interesting that this happens (and I'm

not claiming to be immune from this same confusion when I'm given directions by someone). There are several variables involved as to why this happens, but one is that we often insert our own definitions or interpretations for what we hear or read. ("OK—he did say two miles, but he couldn't have meant exactly two miles. What he must have meant was...")

Do we think we know better what the person means than he does? Are we smarter or more experienced? Is what was said just too literal to be taken seriously—so literal that there has to be some "wiggle room"?

When someone says, "go two miles," what do you think? If you're like me, there is a little variation in your mind. It comes out more "around" two miles than an exact number.

When God says, "Thou shalt not steal," what do we think? Is there a tendency to think only of money and leave out things like "time" in that?

How about, when God says, "Be ye holy for I am holy"? That one leaves little room for wiggling. Holy is the goal because our Lord is holy.

My grandfather used to say, "The Bible says what it means and means what it says." I'll paraphrase that a bit. The Bible says what God means and means what God says. When following His directions, we must be careful to ensure we're not adding to or taking away according to our own interpretation.

*"You have commanded us to keep
Your commandments carefully."*
Psalm 119:4 NKJV

Pursue Wisdom

Sharon and I were checking out the furniture before the auction. As we walked through the aisles, she noticed a beautiful oak chest-of-drawers. She called me over to see it and let me know she loved it. Of course, since she loved it, I did too. So we decided to bid on it and determined what our maximum bid could be.

About an hour into the auction, the workers took the chest to the front of the room. Sharon squeezed my arm and whispered, "There it is!"

The bidding started, and we let a couple of rounds go by before we jumped in. The bids were lower and slower than we expected and were still much below our maximum price. I made a bid that was countered by a slightly higher one. We looked at each other, and since we were still well within our limit, I raised the bid.

I Was Thinking the Other Day About...

We waited excitedly as the seconds ticked by with no other response—then, we really got excited when we heard "sold." The chest was ours for half the cost we thought it would be!

We relaxed and settled back triumphantly to watch more of the auction. The helpers at the front picked up a chest and walked away with it. Then, two others picked up "our" chest and moved it to the center. The auctioneer started with "Now, we have this beautiful oak chest. What am I bid?"

I stood up and started to shout, "Wait, we just bought that one," but I quickly deduced the mistake was ours. We had not been paying attention through most of the auction, and now realized "our" oak chest had been in the waiting area where the items coming up next were placed.

We hadn't even noticed the chest that really was now ours. I had to walk through the aisles of sold stuff and search for our number. I found a plain pine chest of drawers—probably worth what we paid for it—but we had no desire to take it home. We left it there on consignment to be sold at the next auction.

The results of the waylaid process were:

- The pine chest sold at the next auction, but when the auction company took the seller's fee out, we lost money.
- The oak chest sold for about twice what we said

we could afford to pay for it, so our plan wasn't realistic from the beginning.
- We learned the lesson that we need to be sure what we're bidding on before we jump in.

Our pursuit of the chest had gone astray, and it was obvious a pursuit of wisdom would have served us better.

> *"Wisdom is the principal thing;*
> *Therefore, get wisdom..."*
> *Proverbs 4:7 NKJV*

We spend much of our lives pursuing knowledge through school, workshops, reading, and training at work or elsewhere. That's not a bad thing, because knowledge is necessary for what we need and want to do.

The Bible has several passages that emphasize the importance of knowledge. But, as critical as it is, knowledge isn't an end in itself. As the verse above states, we should take knowledge and move beyond it to wisdom. Wisdom is to be our principal pursuit.

It takes wisdom to understand that we need knowledge, and to determine what knowledge we need. It takes wisdom to understand how to use knowledge. A great example of that is Ephesians 4:15 where Paul encourages us to speak the truth in love. Speaking the truth is knowledge. Speaking it in love is wisdom.

It is wise to understand that having more wisdom would be helpful. (As I get older, I am getting wiser, if only because I can see how much more wisdom I need). King Solomon showed that God had given him some wisdom already, because he knew he needed to ask for more. Where does wisdom come from? God does use situations (like auctions) to help us learn wisdom. But, the principal place for us to pursue wisdom is in God's Word, for it is wisdom. Getting wisdom, as stated in the Proverbs verse above, is learning, understanding, and obeying God's Word.

The auction experience did make us wiser (at a cost of money and embarrassment). But, a better way to pursue wisdom isn't through experience. King David wrote in Psalm 119:98-100, that God, through His commandments, had made him wiser than his enemies. Meditating on God's testimonies and obeying God's precepts gave him more understanding than his teachers or his elders.

Then in that same passage, we are given instructions on how we should be guided, not just in our pursuit of wisdom, but in all our pursuits here on earth:

> *"Your Word is a lamp to my feet,*
> *and a light to my path."*
> *Psalm 119:105 NKJV*

Pursue wisdom by the light of God's Word.

Three Reasons to Pump Gas with God

I pushed the button, and the gas pump display read, "See cashier for debit card purchase." I thought about it for half a second, screwed on the gas cap, got back in the truck and drove off in search of a less impudent pump.

Back in the day, before pay-at-the-pump, there was no choice. You went inside the store to pay for your gas. Many people still follow that process and often take the opportunity to get a snack and a cold drink. But, I've developed the habit of just gassing up and going my way and avoiding a trip into the store.

It's usually not that far from the gas pump to the store's checkout, so I don't believe it's laziness on my part. And, if you're not filling up (and having to make the dreaded double trip), the process of going inside usually doesn't take much more time. So it's not from my being in a rush.

No, I think the avoidance comes from the fact that once you go inside the store, you're at the mercy of... people. Is the clerk more concerned with griping to a co-worker about the boss than they are about helping you? Or, is your timing perfect, and you get to wait for a shift change at the cash register? Or, did you manage to hit convenience-store rush hour and there is a line of customers ahead of you?

That afternoon, not long after I headed out in search of the next gas station, I remembered a trip several weeks before. I was traveling through the farms, fields, and forests of rural Georgia. It was a cold, clear, beautiful morning. When it was necessary to stop for gas, I only had one choice in the small town I was passing through. That store didn't have an impudent pump display. It didn't have a display or pay at the pump at all.

So, I stopped at the pump and went inside, wondering what strange happenings would occur to delay my getting back on the road. The clerk said "good morning," and I responded and asked how he was doing. He replied something to the effect of "Great! The Lord has blessed us with a wonderful day."

All aggravation and impatience melted away. I began describing the beautiful sights I had seen and the thankfulness to God I had felt thus far on my morning's journey. As I paid for the gas, we had an enjoyable conversation about the changing season and its contrast to the heat of the summer that was finally ending. I was soon on my way, feeling refreshed from the encounter.

With the memory of that earlier trip in mind, I relaxed in my search for the next station and thought about lessons learned:

- We can bypass some aggravation by avoiding interaction with people. But, doing that causes us to miss many of the blessings of life. It also prevents us being "the light(s) of the world" as Jesus calls us to be. Taking that further, it's when we are acting as Jesus says, that we truly receive the blessings. "In the same way, let your light shine before others, so that they may see your good works and give glory to your Father who is in heaven." Matthew 5:16
- When we are given a lesson, we need to remember it. "My son, do not forget my teaching, but let your heart keep my commandments, for length of days and years of life and peace they will add to you." Proverbs 3:1-2
- And, for me, personally, take a chance the next time the gas pump display tells me to do something I don't want to.

Prime the Pump

The other day an old song came to mind. I don't remember it exactly, but it's a story song with a line that says, "You Have to Prime the Pump." It describes a water pump in a small clump of trees in the desert. It was the old type that you had to pump by hand, and there was a can filled with water hanging from the spout.

For those of you too young to remember, if that type of pump sits for a long time without use, you have to pour water down the pipe in order to make it seal and bring the water up from the ground. That's "priming the pump." The person who would come upon it after having been through the desert would have a strong urge to grab the can and gulp down the water.

But there was a sign on the pump that, in effect, said

"You may be thirsty and want to drink this water, but if you use this water to prime the pump, you can have all you want to drink and plenty more to take with you. And, you can then fill the can for the next person."

So, it really is a song about faith. It would take faith to pour the water into the pump rather than drinking it. It would take faith to look to the future rather than look for a quick drink of water. It would take faith to think of others who would come later and need the water as we did.

The familiar verse of Hebrews 11:1 says: "Now faith is the substance of things hoped for, the evidence of things not seen." (KJV) And, 11:6 says: "But without faith it is impossible to please Him: for he that cometh to God must believe that He is, and that He is a rewarder of them that diligently seek him." (KJV)

We make decisions each day that have short and long-term consequences. We can decide for short-term gratification and take what seems the easy way, or we can decide for the longterm good for others and us. It will always come down to whether we trust in God and are obedient to Him. We must "believe that He is" and diligently seek Him, and He will reward us with "all spiritual blessings in heavenly places in Christ" (Ephesians 1:3).

As the hymn says, we have to "Trust and Obey."

As the Scriptures say, we have to walk by faith.

And, as this old song says, we have to believe enough to "prime the pump."

Pigeons on Power Lines

As I drove past the interchange on I-16, I noticed a flock of pigeons perched on the power line. I didn't count them but guessed there were thirty or more lined up on the wire, just sitting there waiting for something to happen, maybe hoping for a truckload of corn to be accidentally spilled along the highway. ("Bob, do you remember the big corn spill of '07? Boy, what a feast!")

Or, perhaps they were just talking among themselves, passing the afternoon away until it was time to go home to roost. ("Well, I think I'll go home, take a little nap, then go over to Thelma Lou's and watch a little TV.")

The next day my schedule took me back in that direction, and they were in the same place. Since I didn't pay enough attention to recognize any individuals from the day before, I wasn't sure it was the same group, but

I assumed it was. I wondered if they were lined up in the same order as the previous day, like us churchgoers who sit in the same location in the pews each week. ("Hey! Move over—that's my spot!")

I'm not an expert on pigeon perception, but I doubt they noticed me at all. ("Hey Joe, isn't that the same red pickup that came by yesterday?")

The pigeons and I didn't make a connection. I was passing by and happened to see them for an instant. After those few odd thoughts, my brain turned to whatever I was thinking before. They were in their own little world, which didn't include the people passing by on the interstate.

But some people do make connections with pigeons. The owners of homing pigeons easily recognize individual birds. They know each bird's peculiarities in flight, and pickiness in eating. In a race, the owner knows which one will return first and which one will lag behind the others. The connection is made because someone cares enough to invest their time and effort to make it happen.

I'll agree most people won't feel a desire to make connections with pigeons. I may notice them the next time I travel I-16, but I doubt I'll get off the interstate to go introduce myself.

But there is a connection we need to invest time and effort to strengthen—our connection with God. In these busy days, it's too easy to keep trucking down the road, giving only an occasional glance or thought in His direction and then moving on. So let's stop awhile and sit and talk...or maybe, like the pigeons, just sit.

"Be still and know that I am God."
Psalm 46:10

Pecans and the Ox in the Stable

Three huge pecan trees surround our house and each fall, thoughts of gathering the nuts come to mind. There is work involved and some frustrations at times. However, what makes it worthwhile is being able to sell and share some, and put enough in the freezer to have ready for a batch of my wife's banana nut bread.

Nevertheless, last year I found it to be a much easier and less frustrating season. I didn't have to worry about the squirrels being in the trees cutting the nuts down before they were ripe. I didn't have to worry about overstressed limbs falling and leaving a mess to be cleaned up.

Yes, it was much easier—but there was a problem. The squirrels were not there and the limbs weren't breaking because there were no pecans. I didn't even have to work to gather them. It was an easy but fruitless season.

> *"Where there are no oxen, the manger is clean, but abundant crops come by the strength of the ox."*
> *Proverbs 14:4 ESV*

Like the ease of a pecan harvest with no pecans, it's very easy to keep your stable clean if you don't have any oxen in it. In fact, there is probably no work required at all. However, it also means that you don't get the benefit of having an ox to help you do your work. The abundant crops brought by the strength of a helper don't come.

God has called us to good works—and even more emphatic than that, He created us for good works: "For we are his workmanship, created in Christ Jesus for good works, which God prepared beforehand, that we should walk in them." Ephesians 2:10 ESV

The verse states that God has prepared things for our good works. When God provides an ox to help us in those, (in whatever form that "ox" might come), there may be some work and possible frustrations involved. It may require some stable cleaning to perform the good works He has in mind, but we can look forward to the "abundant crops" He will provide.

Mystery Object

The hand-fashioned plywood "For Sale" sign leaned against the over-sized metal object that sat on the side of the road. I called it an object because I had no idea what it was. I was driving to a meeting twenty miles farther down the road, so I made a mental note to look again when I was on my way back home.

As I went by on the return trip, I slowed my truck to get a closer look. While that additional viewing gave me a better idea of what it looked like, I was no closer to knowing what it was. I wondered if there were any people around who might know something about it, but I didn't see any. If there were, my curiosity was such that I would have stopped and asked a few questions.

It wasn't a blade from a bulldozer—I would have recognized that. It looked too heavy to be an implement for a farm tractor. It was worn and rusty from what appeared to be from outdoor use so it probably wasn't a piece of equipment used in a factory.

That day I had been traveling back roads that were lined for miles with tall pine trees, so I made a guess that it must be an attachment for one of the tree harvesters that cut and carry five or six pine trees at one time. But a guess was all it was. Unless I return and the object was still there along with someone to tell me what it was, its identity would remain a mystery.

In Acts, Chapter 8, we read of the Holy Spirit leading Philip to the desert. There he found the Ethiopian eunuch sitting in his chariot reading from the Book of Isaiah. Philip asked if he understood what he was reading, and he replied: "How can I, unless some man should guide me?" Like me, with my inability to identify the mystery object, the Ethiopian needed help to understand the mystery of what he was reading. But, unlike me, who found no one to explain, the Ethiopian did find (through God's leading) the one to answer his questions and tell him about Jesus.

Without the presence of the Holy Spirit, the Gospel is foolishness to a person. His help makes it possible for believers to understand Scripture. However, I'm not aware of anyone that the Holy Spirit has enabled to sit down, read through the Bible once and understand it all. That's why we are told to continue to read, study, and meditate on God's Word.

But, like Philip and the Ethiopian, God also works through other people to help us understand. There are many opportunities for that help—attending Bible Study classes, seeking counsel of godly people around us, and especially hearing God's Word preached.

And, we need to take advantage of all of those opportunities for help, so that we can deal with all the "mysteries" we pass by on our roads of travel.

Lover's Leap for Joy

In this country's mountainous regions there are many locations dubbed "Lover's Leap." They all have associated legends, many involving Native Americans, and with variations on the Romeo and Juliet theme. (Perhaps there is a Lovers' Leap legend in Great Britain and that's where Shakespeare got the idea.)

One legend in the Blue Ridge Mountains of Virginia features a white settler and the Chief's daughter falling in love. After much scorn and exclusion from both families, the couple embrace and plummet to their death to be together forever.

Another tale has a closer semblance to Romeo and Juliet. The two lovers were from different tribes, and members of the maiden's tribe attacked the brave and left him for dead at the top of a cliff. The maiden found him, and thinking he was dead, she jumped off. When he awoke and discovered what had happened, he threw himself over the cliff to be with her.

Jesus refers to a different type of Lover's Leap in the sixth chapter of the Book of Luke:

> "Blessed are you when people hate you and when they exclude you and revile you and spurn your name as evil, on account of the Son of Man! Rejoice in that day, and leap for joy, for behold, your reward is great in heaven; for so their fathers did to the prophets."
> Luke 6:22-23 ESV.

The reactions Jesus describes are also those associated with the Lover's Leap legends: scorn, exclusion, and hatred. The legends end in tragedy, yet Jesus tells us instead of jumping off a cliff, we should respond with a leap for joy.

That is humanly difficult to grasp. We can understand the leap for joy made by those who have been physically crippled their whole life and are miraculously healed by Jesus (and Peter and Paul). However, in this passage, Jesus says we are blessed if we're treated like the ill-fated lovers of the legends. That doesn't sound like a miracle—or does it?

The critical phrase in Jesus' statement is the requirement that our suffering be "on account of the Son of Man." As the Apostle Peter wrote, "what glory is it" if we're hated and scorned because we're hateful and scornful ourselves? No, our enduring this type of suffering is "acceptable to God" and we can leap for joy only because of whom we love: Jesus Christ.

And what's the miracle behind this lover's leap for joy?

"We love Him, because He first loved us."
1 John 4:19

Are We Walking Worthy?

When we see politicians on television news shows, their name is shown at the bottom of the screen so we will know who they are and where they're from ("Representative so and so of this state" or "Senator whoever of that state"). There is usually a (D) or an (R) beside their name, meaning Democrat or Republican, to note their political party.

Sometimes, we don't need to see the D or R to know which party they're in, because they'll be stating opinions and taking positions that are identified with a particular one. At times, they'll be saying or doing things that will make the other people in their party wish that the D or R was not there so they wouldn't be identified with them.

What if television stations started using a (C) after

a person's name to show they are a Christian? If the people in our life—our family, friends, co-workers, and the strangers we deal with along the way—were to see us on the television news giving a sound bite, would there need to be a (C) after our name for them to know that we are a Christian?

Or thinking the other way, if our actions and words were put on the TV screen, and beside our name we did have a (C), would they be surprised to discover we are a Christian? Would other Christians wish we didn't have the (C) there?

Whether we realize it or not, and whether we like it or not, our words and actions are clear signs to those around us. They show where our hearts are, and what we base our life upon.

As Christians, our words and actions should make it evident to others that we are basing our life on Jesus Christ. If we were to be seen on the news with a (C) beside our name, it shouldn't be a surprise or regret to anyone. It would be even better if our faith is so clear that the (C) isn't even necessary.

"I therefore, a prisoner for the Lord, urge you to walk in a manner worthy of the calling to which you have been called."
Ephesians 4:1 ESV

Broken Glass

As I walked through the carport and passed my pickup truck, I noticed several pieces of glass on the concrete. I looked at the side windows and windshields and saw they were intact. A thief once smashed my truck window with a brick so even though I saw no evidence of damage, my first thought was another break-in. I looked around inside to see if anything was missing.

Everything was still there, and as I climbed back out of the truck, I glanced at the driver's side rearview mirror. I saw no image, only black plastic, and so then I realized it was the mirror that had been shattered.

Who would come to the back of our house, walk under the carport and break my mirror? We don't live in a subdivision, and our nearest neighbors live over a quarter of a mile away so it wouldn't likely be someone

I Was Thinking the Other Day About...

wandering around the neighborhood looking to create mischief. It certainly was a mystery.

I retrieved a broom and began sweeping up the remains of the mirror. Among the broken pieces of glass I noticed a small stub of a pecan limb a couple of inches long and about half an inch in diameter. Then the events of the previous day ran through my mind. I had been mowing the overgrown pasture next to our house, and at times the mower would clang and thump as it ran over pecan limbs hidden in the grass.

This small piece must have been a remnant of one of those. It had rocketed from under the mower, sailed over 100 feet and hit the four-inch bull's-eye that was my mirror. A fantastic and nearly impossible shot if I had been trying to make it!

This is the kind of event that we can respond to with anger and aggravation or we can think of ways to be thankful. I could be thankful that the stick broke the mirror instead of a window in the house or the rear windshield on the truck. Both would have been more expensive to replace than the mirror (although my trek to find a replacement mirror may be a story in itself someday.)

I could be thankful the stick didn't hit me and be thankful it didn't hit anyone else. If its flight had not ended when it hit the mirror, the next stop on its trajectory would have been our back porch where someone might have been standing. There definitely were worse possible outcomes than what actually happened.

> *"In everything give thanks..."*
> *1 Thessalonians 5:18 NKJV*

This verse is far deeper than there is space here to discuss and can relate to things far more serious than a broken mirror. One basis to be thankful in everything is that God has promised to be with us in every event in our life—both the serious and the not so serious—and He can be totally trusted for that.

We won't be kept from the trials, but He will take us through them. So, when it comes to everyday aggravations, we can think of things that might have happened, thank the Lord, and say, "If this is the worst thing that happens to me today, it's going to be a wonderful day!"

The Speeding Car

One afternoon, as I was driving home from work, I glanced in my rearview mirror and saw the image of a rapidly approaching car. It quickly caught up, passed, and was soon out of sight ahead of me. I didn't know how fast the driver was going, but my guess would be over eighty miles an hour in a fifty-five-mile-per-hour zone.

The interesting thing I noticed was that as the driver approached, he turned on his left blinker to show that he was passing. Then when he got ahead of me, he turned on his right blinker to show that he was coming back into the lane. I wondered why he bothered to use his turn signals while he was so blatantly breaking the speed limit.

Did he think it made his driving safe because he used

his turn signals? Did he think he had a good reason and needed to break the speed limit, but he was showing how diligent he was in his obedience to signaling a lane change? Did he think he was knowledgeable enough to decide which laws could be broken and then canceled out by obedience to other laws?

Are we, as God's children, sometimes slack on one of His commandments while trying to balance that sin with diligence in obeying others? Do we sometimes think: "I'm not doing well in this part of my spiritual life, but, just look at all the work and obedience I'm showing in that other area"?

God's Word tells us it doesn't work that way. James 2:10 (NKJV) reads:

> *"For whoever shall keep the whole law, and yet stumble in one point, he is guilty of all."*

James doesn't make that statement to say that if we break one of God's commandments we may as well give up. The Bible makes it clear that Jesus is the only person who was able to keep the Law perfectly during His life on earth so that means the rest of us will fail at times. Thankfully, through our faith in Christ, perfection is not demanded of us, but through the strength of the Holy Spirit within us we are expected to work towards obedience in all things.

As we reach towards that goal, James is reminding us that like the driver who couldn't offset his speeding by using his turn signals, we can't cancel sin in one part of our life by getting "extra credit" in another. But rather than giving up because we are not perfect, we can thank the Lord for His grace and strength that have enabled us to be obedient in a particular area, and then ask Him for help and go to work on the areas where we are weakest.

As Charlene Darling Says, Songs Can Make Us Cry

Many years ago, I attempted songwriting. None was worthy of publishing and most mercifully faded from memory. However, there were two I remember (at least the titles). One was a soulful ballad about commitment titled: "If I Don't Leave, Then I Guess I'll Stay." The other was a heart-tugging song about unrequited love: "I Did a Belly-Buster in the Swimming Pool of Love." (Charlene Darling of the old "Andy Griffith Show" would have certainly lamented, "Don't play that one, Pa, it always makes me cry!")

Several years after I wrote those, when our son, Daniel, was still a baby, I made this one up to sing as I tried to get him to sleep (sung to any baby melody you choose):

All the little gophers in gopher town, they all get

together when the sun goes down.

They build a little fire, and dance round and round, all the little gophers in go..pher..town!

The song was still probably not worthy of publishing, but I was pleased with the imagery, and Daniel seemed to enjoy it.

It's difficult to write a good song, especially considering you need to have lyrics and an appropriate melody to go with them. It seems impossible to write a great one. That is one of the reasons so many hymns, old and new, are amazing.

The words touch our hearts with their praise for our great and gracious God, pictures of unshakeable faith, and prayers for God's continuing help. Their accompanying music, whether soaring and broad or simple and quiet, fits perfectly to complement the message.

The background of some of these songs makes them even more amazing. From the well-known story of H.G. Spafford writing "It Is Well With My Soul" on an ocean liner after it passes the spot where his four daughters have recently drowned, to the lesser known circumstances behind Thomas A. Dorsey writing "Precious Lord" after hearing his wife has died in childbirth and the baby has not survived, or Louisa Stead writing "Tis So Sweet to Trust in Jesus" after her husband drowns trying to save a young boy.

As Charlene Darling Says, Songs Can Make Us Cry

These stories reveal the unshakeable faith of the composers. However, above that, especially when considered with the lyrics of the songs themselves, they reveal the love, mercy, and grace of our God.

All the little gophers in gopher town don't really get together and dance around the fire after sundown (at least I don't think they do). But, the Lord's love, mercy, and grace are real. It's shown clearly when we hear—whether we're in peace like a river or in sorrow like a stormy sea—God makes us able to say: "It is well with my soul"; or, we cry out to the Lord to take our hand because we're tired, weary and worn; or we affirm that it truly is sweet to trust in Jesus and know He is with us to the end.

And, when God takes the song and reinforces that reality in our heart at just the right moment and for just the right reason, it can make us cry.

"The LORD is my strength and song,
and is become my salvation."
Psalm 118:14 KJV

Savor the Small Stuff, Too?

Recent sports headlines:

> "Blackhawk rookies have much to savor in victory over Sabres."
>
> "Patriots savor victory a little longer."
>
> "Nets can savor this victory over Pistons."

The other day I walked out the back door, didn't foresee any great victories ahead like those in the headlines, but savored the day ahead anyway. Taking a phrase from Zechariah 4:10, I looked forward to a "day of small things."

> "Then he [an angel] said to me [Zechariah], 'This is the word of the LORD to Zerubbabel: Not by might, nor by power, but by my Spirit,

> says the LORD of hosts. Who are you, O great mountain? Before Zerubbabel you shall become a plain. And he shall bring forward the top stone amid shouts of 'Grace, grace to it!' Then the word of the LORD came to me, saying, 'The hands of Zerubbabel have laid the foundation of this house; his hands shall also complete it. Then you will know that the LORD of hosts has sent me to you. For whoever has despised the day of small things shall rejoice, and shall see the plumb line in the hand of Zerubbabel.'"
> Zechariah 4:6-10 ESV

This passage refers to the time after the Israelites returned to Jerusalem from exile in Babylon. The foundation of the second Temple had been laid, but rather than rejoicing, many of the people were discouraged because it was smaller than Solomon's Temple (which was destroyed during the exile). Those discouraged ones were despising the day of small things.

However, God, in effect, said, "This is just the beginning. Stand back and watch!"—telling them the Temple would be completed and would be the House of God. The Lord had appointed Zerubbabel to lead the construction, and, with the Lord's strength and help, he laid the foundation. Moreover, the victory would come and there would be rejoicing when Zerubbabel lined it up and set the top stone in place.

* * *

The victories in the sports headlines came from many days of small things: Days of practice, running, weightlifting, and sitting there studying their opponent's strengths and weaknesses.

Our lives are also filled with days of small things. But, the exciting part can be that we don't know which of these are the beginnings of victories. We buy seeds and plant a garden. We hold a musical instrument, hammer, or crochet hook for the first time. We meet a new friend. As a writer, we read a Scripture verse, hear a phrase, or see something that gives us an idea. With God's strength and help, these all may lead to victories.

As with Zerubbabel and the rebuilding of the Temple, God often uses small things as the beginnings of His victories: The strings and stakes are laid out for the foundation of a new church. A thought burdens your heart that you should help with a particular ministry, or assist a family in need. An unbelieving friend or relative asks you a sincere question about Jesus.

We can, and should, savor the victories God gives us (and remember all victories are from Him). Nevertheless, a day of small things should be savored, too (and not despised); we need to stand back and watch, because we don't know what great works God has begun that day.

And he [Jesus] said, "With what can we compare the kingdom of God, or what parable

I Was Thinking the Other Day About...

shall we use for it? It is like a grain of mustard seed, which, when sown on the ground, is the smallest of all the seeds on earth, yet when it is sown it grows up and becomes larger than all the garden plants and puts out large branches, so that the birds of the air can make nests in its shade."
Mark 4:30-32 ESV

Really, Really Bad Spring Fever

Spring had been busting out all over for several weeks so spring fever was rampant. I was struggling to stay inside working while the weather was so great. I kept eyeing the postcard that announced the Georgia Southern University Botanical Gardens Spring Festival and Plant Sale was at hand.

The Botanical Gardens hold that on a Saturday but also have a preview sale on Friday for members. Since at the preview, you get first pickings of many unusual plants, I decided to take the afternoon off and take advantage of that.

The postcard said the preview was from 3 to 6 p.m., and I arrived a couple minutes before 3. There were only a few cars in the parking lot, and not many people around. I took a handpulled wagon and started around the tents and lines of plants for sale.

One woman, who also had a wagon, noted we seemed to be playing leapfrog as we took turns moving a little and stopping to check out the plants, while the other went around. There were very few others looking at the plants so I was thinking it was still early, and the crowd would increase as time went on.

The woman stopped her wagon under the checkout tent and told the guy she needed another one and left to get it. I pulled mine next to hers and looked to the "checkout" guy.

"Are you with Susan?" he asked.

"I guess not, since I don't know who Susan is." (I now assume Susan was the woman with the other wagon.)

He looked confused and quizzical and asked if I was a member. I replied that I was and asked, "It was from 3 to 6 wasn't it?"

"Well, it will be that time...tomorrow afternoon."

Wow! Somehow, my spring fever had taken hold enough to make it Friday afternoon in my mind, when it was actually still Thursday.

I apologized and explained that, since I had taken the afternoon off, I apparently started thinking it was Friday already. We worked it out pleasantly, and he was kind enough to allow me to purchase the plants I had loaded in the wagon. As I apologized once more, thanked him, and began leaving, he said "Since it's Friday, don't forget and go into work tomorrow!" We both laughed and parted ways.

Several things worked together to cause my miscue. I work out of our house, and for some reason, in that situation, it's easy to forget what day it is. I also have a one-track mind—I had been debating throughout the week whether to take Friday off, and then I decided to take two afternoons off instead of a whole day, but I guess that wasn't on the track my mind stayed on. However, most of all, I really, really had spring fever, and really, really wanted it to be Friday.

I guess the lesson is that God worked it out for me, even though I wasn't paying attention. We find that happening often, because our God is so gracious and merciful!

> *"Gracious is the LORD, and righteous;*
> *our God is merciful."*
> *Psalm 116:5*

So Fast!

A lady snail was going down the street one day when two turtles came up and snatched her purse. The police asked her if she got a good look at them, and she said, "Why, no, it all happened so fast!"

With this old joke in mind, we can think of situations where things seem to go by fast to us (or perhaps we let them go by). To an outside observer (perhaps God?) there may appear to be plenty of time.

You see friends in a store, or greet them after church. You ask how they're doing, and they say "Fine," but from the tone of their voices and the look on their faces you can tell that's not quite true. But it's time to go and besides, you don't want to intrude, so you reply, "Great! Good to see you," and move on. ("It all happened so fast!")

Someone who is lonely comes to mind during the day and you think, "I need to give her a call." But you're right in the middle of something so you say, "I'll call her later," and the thought leaves as quickly as it came. ("It all happened so fast!")

At work you're talking with someone who is frustrated. He says he doesn't know how you manage to keep your cool in all that's happening. You could tell him that your peace comes from Jesus Christ. But, with all the work you have piled up, you don't really have time to get into a deep conversation right then. So, you make an "I don't know, just lucky I guess" type comment and turn back to your stack of papers. ("It all happened so fast!")

We can probably make a much longer list of times like these when we've let opportunities slip by: opportunities to witness, opportunities to serve, opportunities to show compassion, opportunities to love. From what the Bible says though, God doesn't give us the option of letting them slip by.

> *"Blessed be the God and Father of our Lord Jesus Christ, the Father of mercies and God of all comfort, who comforts us in all our tribulation, that we may be able to comfort those who are in any trouble, with the comfort with which we ourselves are comforted by God."*
> *2 Corinthians 1:3-4 NKJV*

We praise God for the comfort He gives us in our trials. He reveals His mercy and love willingly because that's His character. In the passage above, the Apostle Paul tells us that one reason God offers that is for us to learn from it and then show that same love to others.

We need to watch for the opportunities that God gives us to show His love and take hold of them. Rather than regretfully saying, "It all happened so fast!" we can thankfully say, "It was happening so fast, but by the grace of God, I didn't let it slip by!"

Please, Lord, Make it Real

"Please, Lord, make it real!"

I find myself praying that when I realize all the ways I fall short of where I need (and want) to be. "Real" can mean several positive things, like good, right, pure, strong, or genuine. When I ask God to make it real, I'm not shunning my responsibilities and saying it's all up to Him. I am acknowledging that without His help and power I am helpless to do anything.

Please, Lord, make it real.

Make my anger a righteous anger for Your Name and Your Word, not just pettiness because someone offends me or has a different opinion than I do.

Make my compassion be from the depths of my heart and carried out with action, not shallow and within myself.

Make my passion a passion for Christ and His righteousness, not for material things.

Make my love a willingness to sacrifice with no thought of gain, not a simple emotion in response to others treating me well.

Make my trust in You Rock solid through all times, good and bad, not just an "oh, well" or a "whatever," or only evident when things go well.

The Bible tells of a father who brought his demon-tortured son to Jesus in the hope that He could heal him. He asked that if Jesus were able to do anything, would He have compassion and help them? Jesus replied that if he believed, all things were possible, and the man cried out in tears "Lord, I believe. Help my unbelief" (Mark 9:24 NKJV).

Lord, I believe. Please, make it real in every aspect of my life.

Along and Along

When I was a youngster, I spent several weeks each summer at my uncle's farm in South Georgia. My cousins and I did the fun things people recall from their rural childhoods, like swimming in the creek, and going to town to get a Coke and a Baby Ruth. No, not the old Southern legend Moon Pie, those were good, but a Baby Ruth looked twice as big as the other candy bars. For kids with limited funds, quantity was the deciding factor.

We played baseball in the pasture, and "army" on an abandoned piece of Highway Department land that had the perfect collection of hills, washed-out gullies, and scrub pines to make a great battlefield. However, much of the battle was spent arguing over who would be the Captain.

Nevertheless, fun wasn't the main objective of our days, because my visits always coincided with tobacco harvest season. We spent most of the time "working in tobacco," meaning picking the leaves, stringing them on "tobacco sticks" and hanging them in barns to cure (along with about fifty other parts of the process). Being summer in South Georgia, the temperatures were always in the nineties, and the work was hot and sticky. Not much fun in that.

I wasn't raised on a farm and didn't have many of the skills my cousins had developed through the years. Nevertheless, I did learn as I worked. I thought I was doing quite well when one day I was given the "honor" of hanging the tobacco in the barn.

The tobacco sticks were about four feet long and were hung between parallel "rails" that ran the length of the barn. The sets of rails were vertically spaced a few feet apart from just above head level up to the peaked roof. Typically, there would be four "rooms" of side-by-side sections of rails along the width of the barn.

The hanger straddled between two rails, leaned over and took the tobacco-laden stick from someone below him, and then hung it between the rails above his head. At the upper levels, the height of the barn made it necessary for another person to straddle the rails below the hanger and pass the sticks from someone on the ground up to him.

On my promotion day, two of us climbed from rail to rail and positioned ourselves to start the first room. Other workers took the sticks from the stack outside, passed them through several hands, and finally to me. I concentrated on getting the correct spacing between sticks and on remembering I couldn't just walk on air to the next spot.

We finished the upper levels of the first and second rooms and were nearing completion of the third when my older cousin came in. He was the "boss" that day and in his boss voice he barked, "What happened up top?"

Before I replied, he scrambled up the rails, scowling and grumbling as he passed me. I soon heard: "You missed the peak on these two sections!" I climbed up and saw he was right. The two tiers at the peaks of the second and third rooms were a void among the tobacco-filled space below them.

I could have argued there wouldn't be that many sticks in those sections, but that was useless. That space represented money. It took a certain amount of propane to cure a barn of tobacco, so the more product in there, the less cost per pound. Also, an open section at the top could affect the consistency of the curing, and thus affect the selling price.

He had us start shifting the already hung sticks to make room for him to work. It was like one of those

I Was Thinking the Other Day About...

little tile picture puzzles with fifteen tiles and one space. You move a tile over in the corner and work your way one by one to the piece you really want to move.

The process of making room, hanging the peaks, and re-hanging the area around them took an extra thirty minutes (but seemed like two hours). My cousin did allow me to continue hanging the fourth room (after he hung the peak). But, I could tell he had been aggravated by the delay and rework.

I didn't know how I missed the extra space. I continued to silently bemoan my mistake as we finished the barn. My face must have revealed regret as I moped around while we were getting ready to go back to the house. As my cousin noticed my forlorn look, he flashed a big grin and said: "Don't worry, we'll learn ya' along and along!" I mirrored his grin as my anguish melted away.

They continued to do as he said. Each summer they taught me more of the tasks involved in farming. While I wouldn't consider myself an expert in any of it, I think I did OK for a "city" boy.

The Apostle Paul wrote of doing things he shouldn't do, and not doing things he should do. From reading about Paul's life after his conversion, that is hard to imagine, but it does show that even the most faithful of God's children aren't born again into instant perfection.

We go through a lifelong process, often failing as Paul mentions, but also, when we are faithful and obedient, we grow and improve, and walk closer with God. Thankfully, it isn't our power, but the power of God that takes us on that journey so that we can "fight the good fight" and "run the race." Moreover, as Paul also wrote, we can be assured that God will complete His good work in us.

"Being confident of this very thing, that He which hath begun a good work in you will perform it until the day of Jesus Christ."
Philippians 1:6 KJV

The South Georgia translation of that could be: "Don't worry, He'll learn ya' along and along."

In Summary

I mentioned in the introduction that I hoped these stories would cause the reader to think about God, and aid in the journey closer to Him.

I ended with "Along and Along" to emphasize that God is intimately involved in that journey. He uses the happenings in our life, good and bad, small and large, to show us His love and mercy, and teach us how we should live.

Finally, I'll restate my mission statement, not as a mission statement for all, but as encouragement along the journey.

All that really matters in life are God and other people. So act like it.

Do the right things for the right reasons.

Pay Attention!

More about the Author

Bill Jones grew up in Statesboro, Georgia, which is about 60 miles west of Savannah. His wife, Sharon, is also from there, and they have been together since they were high school sweethearts. Now, they are in their 40th year of wedded bliss.

Their son, Daniel, and daughter-in-law Stephanie, are at Cambridge University (UK) where Daniel is an oceanographer. With that, Bill and Sharon's two year old grandson, Alex, is a long way from Gammy and Grandpa.

Bill is, by trade, an electrical engineer (graduated from Georgia Tech) and has spent his career in the electric utility business, mainly in Savannah, Georgia. He and Sharon lived in Savannah for a time, and then moved "to the country" about half way between Savannah and Statesboro.

They now live on a dirt road surrounded by fields and forests. (Daniel often referred to it as the middle of nowhere). That gives Bill the perfect location for gardening (his favorite hobby) and enjoying, and observing God's creation.

While Bill has had articles posted in magazines, and his thinking has been present most of his life, much of his writing has come about following his and Sharon's volunteering several years ago to publish their church's monthly newsletter. He began writing a monthly column that has the same title and focus as this book, and from which many of the stories got their start.

Bill's writing has branched out to the internet and he has been writing a blog for the past several years. Many of the posts focus on gardening and the wonder of God's Creation, but other stories make it in, and the humor and unique perspectives seen in this book are still there. The blog is "I Was Thinking the Other Day About..." (at www.iwasthinkingtheotherday.com.)

www.ingramcontent.com/pod-product-compliance
Lightning Source LLC
Chambersburg PA
CBHW071502040426
42444CB00008B/1458

"We'll learn ya along and along"

What Biblical lessons can you learn from falling out of your uncle's pickup truck, accidentally hitting your cousin in the eye with a paddleball, or watching toads patiently wait for tasty bugs? Bill Jones pondered those, and other memories and observations of everyday life, and found the lessons God gives in them. Such thinking crystallized his understanding that God's goodness and greatness are all around us, and He is with us every step of our journey through life.

The stories told in these devotional readings illustrate how God uses the happenings in our life, both the good and bad, and the small and large, to show us His love and mercy, and teach us how we should live. Mixing touches of humor and unconventional perspectives, the author gives us the opportunity to do some thinking about our great and gracious God, and, hopefully, get a little closer to Him.

BILL JONES and his wife, Sharon, live in a rural area of southeastern Georgia where they attend a small community church. He has had inspirational articles published in *Evangel*, *Keys to Living* and *The Christian Journal* magazines.